Co

Fish

Michael Prichard
illustrated by Keith Linsell

HarperCollins Publishers Ltd.
77-85 Fulham Palace Road
London
W6 8JB

The Collins website address is:
www.collins.co.uk

Collins is a registered trademark of
HarperCollins Publishers Ltd.

First published in 1986
This edition published 2004

Text © Michael Prichard
Illustrations © Keith Linsell, except for pp. 49, 108, 173, 174, 175, 187
© Michael J. Loates, and p..86 © HarperCollins

10 09 08 07 06 05

10 9 8 7 6 5 4 3 2

A catalogue record for this book is available from the British Library.

ISBN 0 00 718013 6

Designed by Penny Dawes
Edited by Kate Parker
Printed and bound in Italy by Amadeus S.r.l.

CONTENTS

INTRODUCTION

What is a fish?

For centuries considerable confusion existed concerning the true definition of the word. Most people thought that anything living in water had to be a fish. Others thought that the possession of fins was a necessary qualification, but this thinking was still wrong because it brought fish and mammals into the same group of creatures.

Fish can be simply defined as creatures that live all of their lives in water, are cold-blooded, take in oxygen from the surrounding water through gills, do not exhibit placentation (except of a very primitive kind, in certain instances) and cannot suckle their young. Aquatic mammals, such as whales and seals, do have fins with which to move but they also have warm blood, grow their own young in a uterus and suckle for a protracted period. Higher mammals also teach their juveniles family and social behaviour. There is little if any parental care by most male or female fish, although some species do build nests and guard both the eggs and hatching fry. Usually spawning is on a haphazard basis, with fish broadcasting their eggs and milt in the surrounding water. The eggs are then left to survive as best they can!

Prehistory

Fish appeared on the earth millions of years ago, long before the animals that we recognise today existed. At that time most creatures lived in water. Some air-breathing creatures, such as the dinosaurs, needed water to support their massive bulk. Fish, although possessing rudimentary limbs, have never lived permanently on the land mass. It would seem that most fish are perfectly adapted to the medium in which they live.

The selachians arrived first, followed by two other groups of fish: the bony fish, and the lampreys and hagfish. The former group has by far the greatest number of species, living in both fresh and saltwater. Although vertebrates, not all fish possess a bony skeleton, however. Some species, notably the sharks and skates, have a skeletal structure composed of gristly cartilage. These groups of fish are of much older origin than the true bony fish. Scientists will tell you that, strictly speaking, only the bony fish can be truly termed 'fish'. For purposes of identification, we will consider them all as true fish.

Much of what we know about the early forms of fish has been learned from fossil remains. Some splendid examples exist, in natural history museums,

Fossil

which indicate that few changes in skeletal make-up
have occurred over the passage of time.

Classification of fish

Classification, of the world of nature, means sorting
all animals and plants into groups that have similar
characteristics. The simplest unit of classification is
the species. Varieties within a species, such as Mirror
Carp, do not constitute a sub- or separate species. A
number of similar, closely related species come
together to form a genus (plural genera). Individual
genera form families which are further grouped
into sub-orders and orders. A number of orders will
constitute a sub-class or class which, in turn, join
sub-kingdoms and kingdoms.

Often there will be a name following the generic name. This is the sponsor or discoverer, who would have described the animal for the first time. If that name appears in brackets, it means that the species has since been put into a different genus from that ascribed by the original classifier. Both names are in Latin or Latinised Greek.

Example: Porbeagle Shark

Species: **Lamna nasus**
Genus: **Lamna**
Family: **Lamnidae**
Order: **Lamniformes**
Sub-class: **Elasmobranchii**
Class: **Chrondrichthyes**

It was the Swedish naturalist Linnaeus – in his Systema Naturae, a book written in 1758, which has become the ichthyologist's bible – who devised this system.

How to identify a fish

Fish can be identified by asking a series of questions
concerned with how the fish looks externally:

1 Size and shape of the body

To make an accurate identification, first ask the
question: 'Is the fish large or small?' Then, 'Is it round,
or flat?' Establishing the shape of a particular fish
will lead to a narrowing down of the field to
sensible proportions. With many species there is a
marked size difference between male and female.

2 Position and number of fins, and whether spined or soft

Fins are important limbs of locomotion and their
number and position on the fish's body changes
from one species to another. Some fish, the Cod for

Anatomy of the Perch

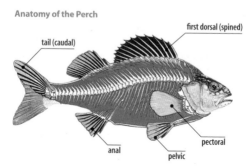

tail (caudal)

first dorsal (spined)

pectoral

anal

pelvic

example, have three dorsal fins. So, seeing or catching a marine fish with that number of fins will put it into the cod family, which narrows down the identification search.

3 Possession of teeth and their type

All fish have teeth, but they aren't always apparent! Freshwater Carp have throat teeth called pharyngeals for grinding food items. They are positioned at the entrance to the Carp's gullet. Sharks have vicious teeth that can be clearly seen as instruments for cutting and tearing flesh. The Whiting has a mouth full of tiny, sharp teeth intended for grasping and trapping smaller fish, on which it feeds. Having numerous sharp teeth usually establishes a predator.

4 Type of skin or scales and the number that can be counted in a defined area

Fish have skin into which scales are embedded. Sometimes the scales are large, soft and easily seen. These are described as being cycloid. There are some species that have minute scales which appear almost as smooth skin. Over the scales there is usually a coating of protective slime, acting as a barrier to water and preventing access to infection. The Sea Bass has scales that are hard, with a raised point on the rear edge. These are called ctenoid.

Many reference books advise you to count the
number of scales along the fish's lateral line; this is a
clearly defined line of scales along each side of the
body which acts as a sensory organ, enabling the
fish to feel vibrations and gauge its proximity to
underwater obstructions. Counting scales will work
admirably with fish of one species. But, in freshwater
certainly, there may well be a degree of
hybridisation between a number of closely-related
species that inhabit the same water space. Hybrids,
though strongly resembling one of the parent fish,
will have a peculiar scale count.

5 Colour or skin scales

The colour of skin or scales cannot be used as an
isolated identification point. The body colour of a
fish may well depend of the colour of the
environment, and whether the habitat is well lit or
very dark. Rock Codling are a splendid example of
fish take on the rich, reddish hue, similar to the kelp-
strewn habitat in which they live. In earlier times, the
Brown Trout was thought (because of its many
colour variants) to be a number of different species,
depending on where it was found. The truth is that
habitat often conditions colour and, to a lesser
extent, the body shape of the fish. Even fish that are
hardly ever confused with near relatives, such as the
Tench, can produce confusing colaborations.

Cuckoo Wrasse are one species in which there is a year-round difference in colour between sexes. A near relation, the Ballan Wrasse, displays a fantastic array of colourings among a collection of individuals coming from the same habitat. Both of these situations have led anglers and naturalists into thinking that they were inspecting different species, rather than species/sexual colour variants.

6 **Possession of thorns, spurs, barbules, tubercles, coloured patches, visible sexual appendages or any other noticeable characteristics**
When looking at a catch of rays some will have distinctive spots and others may have sharp thorns. The position and type of markings or thorns will give the clue to the species – the overall colour can and does alter.

Among the larger sea fish subtle external features are more easily detected. The lateral keels of the Porbeagle Shark are pronounced and make a useful identification point. Spurdogs and smoothhounds are somewhat alike until one looks closely at fins and mouths. The large, sharp spine that precedes both dorsal fins on the Spurdog give the fish its name. Inspecting the mouth and teeth can help when trying to arrive at a name. Smoothhounds are members of the same group of fish as the Spurdog but they feed on different animals.

Internal organs of the female Cod

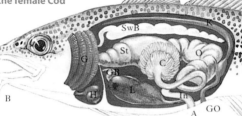

G: gills
H: heart
SwB: swim bladder
St: stomach
K: kidney
O: ovary
In: intestine

A: anus
GO: genital opening
L: liver
GB: gall bladder
C: cloaca
B: barbule

Male Spurdog

Spn: spleen
In: intestine
P: pancreas
L: liver
H: heart

T: testis
K: kidney
St: stomach
Sp: spine

Their teeth are of a flat, grinding kind, used to crush crabs and other small crustaceans. The small, needle-like teeth of the Spurdog are intended to grasp pelagic shoalfish as they try to escape in the upper water layers.

Sharks, skates and rays have visible, external differences. Male fish have a pair of elongated claspers, used when copulating. Each of these families of fish vary from the bony fish in that the females are fertilised internally.

A final identification check is to ask yourself whether a particular fish ought to be in its immediate habitat. Finding a Flounder high up in a river is not unusual, for this marine species is highly tolerant of freshwater and annually ascends into rivers to feed. However, beware of identifying it as a Plaice because of the orange spots that may be on the body. The Plaice is similar in shape but is a totally marine species that would never be found in freshwater.

Freshwater fish also have their habitat preferences. The Rudd is unlikely to be found in a fast-flowing stream, but its close relative, the Roach, which looks remarkably similar, would be far more likely to inhabit the stream.

A NOTE ON THE TEXT

There are about 20,000 species of fish spanning the fresh- and saltwaters of the world. About 5,000 species live in freshwater, and a few, such as salmon, sturgeon and eels, move periodically between the two conditions. This guide covers marine species of the north-east Atlantic, and freshwater species of Britain and western Europe.

The order in which the fish are presented in this book follows Linnaeus's system of classification (see also p. 8). Side headings on each page will help to identify any 'family' groupings. Unfortunately, over the years many fish have been given a mass of local or regional names which add to the difficulty of identification. In this volume I have tried to simplify an incredible variety of popular names by referring to each fish by only one or occasionally two names.

Sizes of fish vary enormously from area to area and due to environmental factors such as food supply. However, I have given approximate maximum measurements to allow some comparison between species. A large number of fish lengths have been taken from *Collins Pocket Guide: Fish of Britain and Europe* by Peter J. Miller and Michael J. Loates (1997). The marine species' weights have been derived from The Irish Specimen Fish Committee's Report for the Year 1999 – Record Fish Listing. These are realistic weights for the various species. Those for the freshwater fish have come from a wide variety of sources because many species are absent in Ireland.

Coloration is mentioned chiefly to identify a species of fish from a closely related one rather than being routinely included in each 'Appearance' subsection. The pictures themselves provide an accurate record of colouring in each case. Because little information is available for many species of fish, details of breeding, distribution and even feeding cannot always be given.

Finally, it should be noted that, while I draw attention to those fish most sought after for the table, all the fish recorded here are edible. Indeed, the uglier the fish, generally the more delicate the flesh – the Monkfish, John Dory and Red Gurnard being prime examples!

THE FRESHWATER ENVIRONMENT

Water both supports the bodies of fish and provides oxygen to sustain life, while allowing fish to move about. Water is continuously supplied as rain, or snowmelt from mountains. Oxygen is a constituent part but it can also be added by wind ruffling the surface of a pond, when water falls, such as over a weir sill, or when a tiny stream rushes down a steep gradient. Oxygen is also introduced into the water by water plants, by a process known as photosynthesis.

Fish like clean water in which to live, feed and reproduce. Various species have different oxygen demands. Brown Trout (*Salmo trutta*) look for a high oxygen content, whereas Carp (*Cyprinus carpio*) can live in situations that offer a very low amount. Some fish are more tolerant than others of poor-quality water but few fish can survive the serious pollution, in the form of vast amounts of manmade toxic substances and effluent from farms, which constantly pours into lakes and rivers. Nobody really knows why different species prefer to live in fresh or saltwater. Some, such as members of the salmon family, move easily from one to the other and back again. It is

A still water in summer

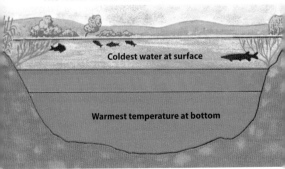

Epilimnion (warmest)

Thermocline (band of changing-temperature water)

The water in mid-winter

Coldest water at surface

Warmest temperature at bottom

possible for fish to adapt, too; for instance, most of the beautiful fish we keep as aquarium pets came, originally, from saltwater environments.

Fish will select areas, in any piece of water, to suit their lifestyle, varying their habitat by periodic moves to find food either as an individual fish or as a member of a shoal or age group. There may be seasonal migration to breed, to escape predators or to seek suitable temperatures. Juvenile fish may even wish to depart from an area that holds adults of their own species; in short, they are always looking for comfortable surroundings. Fish found in rivers display slightly different migratory behaviour to members of the same species that live in still water. Water temperature has less effect in rivers, as the heating-up and cooling-down processes are much slower.

RIVER LAMPREY *Lampetra fluviatilis*

A primitive vertebrate with a cartilaginous structure, a rudimentary gill formation, and no gill cases or swim bladder.

Appearance Length 50 cm. Scaleless, eel-shaped body with no paired fins. Mouth a circular disc with a single row of horny teeth that grip the body of another fish, enabling the lamprey to suck the blood of its victim. Dorsal fins of breeding fish become larger.

Breeding Adult fish migrating upriver from the sea to spawn. Spawning during Feb–June in furrows or holes, made by the male fish, on stony gravel bottoms; after spawning the adult fish die. Many thousands of eggs, which hatch in a few weeks into blind, toothless larvae that burrow into the mud of the riverbed. After 2–5 years, they metamorphose into the true lamprey shape and make their way to the sea to grow to adult size.

Distribution Rivers of Britain and Europe and the surrounding oceans.

SEA LAMPREY   *Petromyzon marinus*

Like the River Lamprey (see p. 20), this is a primitive invertebrate that lives by sucking the blood of other fish. See River Lamprey for Breeding.

Appearance Length 90 cm. Similar to the River Lamprey but the mouth has multiple rows of teeth instead of a single row.

Feeding As an adult, living in coastal waters, the lamprey of both species feeds on Sea Trout, Shad and Whitefish.

Distribution Found on both sides of the North Atlantic and into the western Mediterranean coastal waters.

STURGEON

Acipenser sturio

The Sturgeon, though rarely seen, can grow to a huge size and is widely known as the fish that provides us with caviar. It is one of at least 16 species in the Northern Hemisphere. The membrane of the swim bladder is used commercially to create isinglass, a gelatine used in the production of confectionery and the refining of alcoholic drinks.

Appearance Length can exceed 300 cm; weight can be up to 282 kg. Long and streamlined body with five rows of hard, bonelike plates (scutes). Head also protected by a shield of scutes. Four barbules in a line across the underjaw. Pointed snout and a small, often protruding mouth. Powerful tail with a larger upper lobe. Remaining fins quite small when compared to the size of the body.

Feeding Feeds by rooting around in the soft mud of the sea and riverbed for small food items, including fish such as minnows.

Breeding Travels far up into freshwater to spawn. Breeds in the spring, in rivers with pebble beds. More than 1 million eggs are shed. After hatching the young fish remain in freshwater for up to three years.

Distribution From northern Russia, around the Atlantic coast, into the Mediterranean and the Black Sea.

ALLIS SHAD

Alosa alosa

A herring-like fish, said to be anadromous, living most of its life in saltwater, yet migrating into freshwater to breed, before returning to the sea. The lateral line, normally visible on most round fish, is poorly represented in both this and the Twaite Shad (see p. 25).

Appearance Length 30–40 cm; weight 1 kg. Slender, silver body with dark blue back and a possible row of black spots along its flanks. It can have one large blotch behind the gill case with further paler spots behind it and a mass of dense gill-rakers, over 100 on first gill arch.

Feeding Minute plankton.

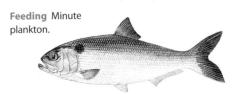

Breeding Spawns many eggs in spring which usually hatch within two weeks. Juvenile fish may stay in the river for 12 months or more, before descending with the current to the sea.

Distribution Around the North Atlantic coast, from Norway to Portugal.

TWAITE SHAD *Alosa fallax*

Like the Allis Shad (p. 24), this is a herring-like, anadromous fish. Neither species has any real economic importance, although they are trapped in estuary nets as they enter freshwater on their annual, spring spawning migration.

Appearance Length 55 cm; weight 1.45 kg. Dark blue on the back, fading to bronze-yellow flanks with 6–10 blotches behind the gill case and about 50 gill-rakers on the first gill arch.

Feeding Minute plankton and larger fish fry.

Breeding Spawning take place in May, often at night. See also Allis Shad.

Distribution More widespread than the Allis Shad, it can be found offshore and entering rivers in places as far apart as Norway and Turkey.

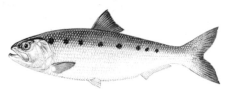

ATLANTIC SALMON

Salmo salar

Now a common food due to the proliferation of fish farms, mostly along western coasts of our shores. These farms produce thousands of tons of fish per year.

Appearance Length 153 cm. Streamlined, powerful body with blue-black back, silver sides and creamy-white underbelly. In freshwater, both adult sexes change into a breeding pelage, becoming more reddish. Male fish grows a kype – a hooked underjaw – often so extended that it cannot close its mouth. Parr have black back and dark vertical bars over bright silver scales dotted with reddish spots.

Feeding Do not feed in freshwater, relying totally on food (chiefly Cod) eaten at sea to get them through breeding. After breeding few adult fish ever get back to the sea. Many die in upriver pools, while a few fish drop down on the current flow to saltwater, where they make their way back to the established feeding grounds.

Breeding In freshwater, high upstream in the headwaters of pure, cool, highly oxygenated rivers. In

late autumn or early winter, the female
constructs a redd. She
scrapes a hollow in
the gravel of a fast-
flowing shallow and
spawns in it. Then
she covers the
fertilised eggs by
fanning the loose gravel with her tail.

The male guards against the arrival of other breeding
pairs that would rip up the earlier-spawned eggs.

Eggs hatch in 90–130 days, depending on water
temperature. The newly emerged alevins feed on the
yolksac. They gradually develop from fry to parr and
forage for plankton, growing quickly in the warming
water. Some stay in freshwater for only one year; they
then change their colouring, becoming silvery smolts,
and leave for the sea. Others remain for up to three
years in the river. Salmon may return to the river they
were spawned in after growing in oceanic waters. A
fish that returns after only one year is called a grilse. The
British Rod Caught Record is a fish of 29 kg.

Distribution The North Sea, Atlantic and Arctic
oceans and the rivers of Britain, Scandinavia, Greenland
and Iceland. Some rivers in northern Spain have a run
of salmon as do a few rivers in Russia.

BROWN TROUT   *Salmo trutta fario*

Among the best of sporting fish, it enjoys a worldwide reputation for its fight and as a valuable food resource, which has been farmed extensively for many years. Although primarily a fish of the Northern Hemisphere, the Brown Trout has been introduced to a variety of habitats in many countries. Successful living and breeding depend largely on water quality.

As members of the salmon family, Trout should demand water conditions of purity and high oxygenation. In reality the species is to be found in a wide variety of waters, some of doubtful water purity. Brown Trout are found in rivers and in still waters, both in the headwaters of a highland river as well as far down in the middle, slow-running reaches. Even in estuaries, the Slob Trout (a Brown Trout that prefers to hunt in brackish water) is often taken in nets: sufficient evidence that the fish can tolerate salt and brackish water.

Appearance Length 80 cm; weight 5 kg. Great variety in coloration. Typically, the back is a rich, green-brown, lightening to creamy-brown flanks and a yellow belly. Trout of all ages are richly spotted. Both sexes display black and red spots on the gill cases and body, becoming fewer towards the tail fork. Red spots have a fringing of creamy white. Scales are small and smooth.

Feeding Feeds on insects and small invertebrates, especially in the still waters of highly fertile limestone regions, and the fry of other species of fish.

Breeding From late autumn into early the following year. The female becomes mature at three years old, the male a year earlier. Trout move from deep water, in rivers or lakes, to gravelly shallows in fast-flowing feeder streams, where the female fish scrapes a redd among the small stones. After fertilisation, the eggs are covered in the gravel, where they hatch in eight weeks, with a water temperature of about 6°C.

Distribution Basically a European species, it can be found from Iceland to northern Spain, although there are some Brown Trout in both the Black and Caspian seas.

female

male

SEA TROUT

Salmo trutta trutta

Appearance Length 140 cm; weight 6.5 kg. Similar to Atlantic Salmon in shape (see p. 26), but with smaller silver scales that give a sleek appearance. Tail is nearly squared off with no apparent fork. Small black spots cover the body above the lateral line. Upper bone of the mouth extends beyond the eye, whereas that of the larger salmon ends at the rear edge of the eye.

Feeding See Brown Trout (p.28). Parr eat tiny larval water insects and invertebrates.

Breeding Similar spawning environment to the Brown Trout. It is said that the two varieties of fish can interbreed successfully.

Distribution North Sea and Atlantic and Arctic oceans. Like the Brown Trout, Sea Trout have been introduced by sportsmen to many lands, notably New Zealand, Australia, South Africa and South America.

RAINBOW TROUT   *Salmo gairdneri*

The Rainbow Trout was introduced from North America and is today stocked all over Europe as an angling and fish-farming species, but does not really succeed as a wild breeding species here. It grows quickly, but is artificially spawned for a higher fecundity. See Brown Trout (p. 28) for Breeding. Distribution is artificial.

Appearance Length 100 cm. Small, colourful scales give the Rainbow Trout its name.

Feeding Feeds on insects and small invertebrates, especially in the still waters of highly fertile limestone regions, and the fry of other species of fish.

ARCTIC CHAR   *Salvelinus alpinus*

An anadromous fish of northern seas and rivers, the Arctic Char is land-locked in British waters. It is thought to be an example of remnant arctic fauna, left by the retreating ice of the last ice age. Like all members of the salmon group, Arctic Char make splendid eating.

Appearance Length 60 cm. Males highly colourful at spawning time. Small body scales are predominantly silver; large reddish spots on back and flanks.

Feeding Small fish, molluscs and invertebrates.

Breeding Spawning takes place in late winter on pebble beds, with male fish sometimes guarding the redds.

Distribution In the larger waters of the Lake District and small loughs in mountainous regions of Ireland. This fish can also be found in Russia and northern lakes of America and Canada.

BROOK TROUT

Salvelinus fontinalis

Like the Rainbow Trout (see p. 31), the Brook Trout was introduced to Europe from North America, but it is in fact a char. Brook Trout tolerate high water temperatures, so can be stocked into lowland fisheries, although in America it inhabits cold highland streams. Being a farmed fish, distribution is artificial.

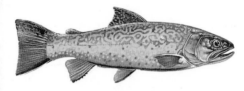

Appearance Length 66 cm. Dark-greenish body with curling lines of light colour giving a marbled appearance. Like the Arctic Char (see p. 32), males change into a bright pelage at spawning time lasting through late autumn and early winter.

Feeding Insects and the parr of other species.

Breeding Nests are made in stony river and streambeds. After spawning the eggs are covered and will hatch in the early spring.

WHITEFISH   *(Coregonus lavaretus)*

A collection of minor members of the salmon family, all whitefish are declining, as a breeding stock, in European waters. The Powan, Schelly and Gwyniad (all *Coregonus laveratus*) are thought to be derived

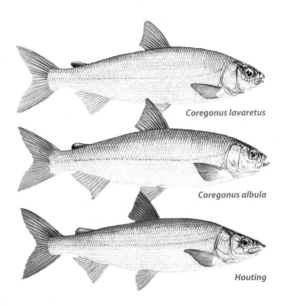

Coregonus lavaretus

Coregonus albula

Houting

from the Houting, the only member of the group that is sea-going. The Vendace, *Coregonus albula*, also belongs to this group of Coregonoids and is commercially netted for food in eastern Scandinavia (Finland) and Russia.

Appearance 50–70 cm. All species are silvery, with fairly large scales and an adipose fin. Identification is not easy as there are similarities between species and taxonomists disagree upon scientific names.

Feeding Larvae, small crustaceans and the young of other species.

Breeding Breed on beds of gravel and small stones in the autumn.

Distribution Powan inhabit Loch Lomond. Schelly are fish of the Lake District and the Gwyniad belongs to a few Welsh waters. Vendace have their home in Loch Maben and Lough Neagh and Houting are found in estuaries in northern and eastern Britain and are widely, though thinly, distributed in the Baltic.

GRAYLING
Thymallus thymallus

One of nature's most beautiful fish, the Grayling has a characteristic smell, like that of the garden herb thyme.

Appearance Length 60 cm. Graceful, lean body covered in bright silver scales; horizontal purplish stripes along the flanks. Pronounced dorsal fin acts like a giant sail, helping to establish the fish in its chosen resting place.

Feeding Regarded as a competitor for food by Trout fishery owners, the Grayling also feeds on items ignored by trout, for example crustaceans and larvae.

Breeding Spawns in the spring, unlike other members of the salmon tribe, depositing many eggs in a shallow redd. The male fish wraps his huge dorsal fin across the female as the eggs are fertilised. The eggs hatch quicker and the fry grow much faster than the native trout that inhabit the same environment.

Distribution Found throughout northern Europe but only locally in Britain.

SMELT

Osmerus eperlanus

A species that can equally well survive in fresh or saltwater, the Smelt hatches in freshwater, spends most of its life feeding at sea but returns to breed in a river. When freshly caught, this fish smells faintly of cucumber!

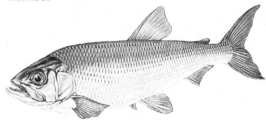

Appearance Length 46 cm. Small and slender in shape, with tiny defined scales and a mouth that appears too large for the body.

Feeding Larvae and fry of other species of fish.

Breeding Breeds in spring, choosing a sandy or gravelly bottom often in the inter-tidal zone.

Distribution Found from the Bay of Biscay to the Baltic Sea.

PIKE

Esox lucius

Loved by many naturalists but sometimes despised as a ruthless predator, the Pike performs a vital function in freshwater. These fish are the 'regulators' for many still waters and rivers, ensuring that the environment does not become overcrowded or contain masses of stunted and ailing fish. But they only take sizable fish, whereas trout are responsible for massive predation among the eggs and fry of most species. There is one genus and only one represented species in European waters, although Esox has close relatives in Asia and North America.

Many tales are told about 'monster' Pike; some have foundation because the Pike will grow in direct ratio to the amount of fodder fish present in its territory. This species does not have to be old to grow large. A female Pike of over 22.7 kg and just over eight years old was netted from Lough Mask. Loch Lomond, along with many of the other large lakes of the British Isles, is legendary for the enormous Pike that it holds.

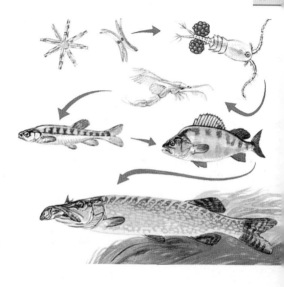

Appearance Length 90 cm (male), 150 cm (female); weight 17 kg. A sleek, powerful body and large tail enable the Pike to move very fast over short distances. Binocular vision also helps the fish judge the distance between itself and its prey. Superbly camouflaged, green-bronze colouring over the body, shading to a creamy-white belly. Lighter, regular marblings of yellow on the flanks with smaller spots above the lateral line. Paired fins are small. Large head with a marked extension of the lower jaw and a huge number of teeth, the larger ones for gripping prey. The dense pattern of teeth on the roof of the mouth act as a one-way trap: a fish can get in but not out. The meal is grabbed crosswise, then turned and swallowed.

Feeding Smaller Pike, up to 15–23 cm, feed on minute larvae and other water creatures found in the shallow areas of lakes or running waters. Larger Pike eat live and dead fish, amphibians, small water mammals and birds. Also cannibalistic – known to eat other Pike of similar size.

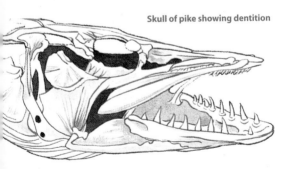

Skull of pike showing dentition

Breeding From early February to April, Pike move to shallow breeding areas with heavy weed growth, to which they return each year. Each female is accompanied by a number of smaller males. Note that all large Pike are female, male fish rarely exceeding 4–5 kg in weight. Eggs are shed among the weedfronds and hatch in 10–40 days, depending on water temperature. The minute larvae attach themselves to weed, where over 10 days they absorb the yolksac and gills and fins develop. They then become free-swimming and begin feeding on plankton.

Distribution Throughout the rivers and still waters of Europe.

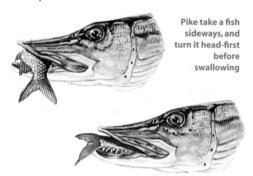

Pike take a fish sideways, and turn it head-first before swallowing

ROACH

Rutilus rutilus

The Roach belongs to the carp family Cyprinidae, which is the biggest family of fish on earth and is the most widespread freshwater fish in Britain. Roach are found in all types of water environment but are best suited to a clean, fast-flowing stream where they develop hard, lean bodies with superb coloration. They are a shoal fish, often found in size/age groups that seem to remain as a unit until the breeding season, when they mix with other groups and fish of other species.

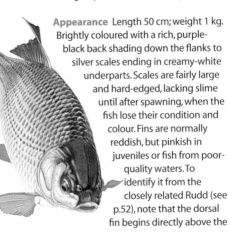

Appearance Length 50 cm; weight 1 kg. Brightly coloured with a rich, purple-black back shading down the flanks to silver scales ending in creamy-white underparts. Scales are fairly large and hard-edged, lacking slime until after spawning, when the fish lose their condition and colour. Fins are normally reddish, but pinkish in juveniles or fish from poor-quality waters. To identify it from the closely related Rudd (see p.52), note that the dorsal fin begins directly above the

pelvic fins, whereas the Rudd's starts well behind these. The Roach has a slightly longer top jaw; the Rudd's underjaw is longer.

Feeding Larvae, insects, small crustaceans, worms.

Breeding Spawns in the spring when the water temperature rises above 14°C. Males become brighter in colour and mature males develop small white breeding tubercles on the head and sides. Sticky eggs are deposited in shallow, slow-flowing backwaters and adhere to weed fronds. They hatch in about a week, and the minute larvae adhere to the weeds for 2–3 days, after which the fry cluster in huge clouds to escape predation by small pike and perch.

Distribution Found in both running and still waters from the south of England up to the Scottish Highlands. Introduced to Ireland in the early 1900s, the Roach has spread from the Cork Blackwater and Ulster Erne to many other connected river systems. A number of allied species on the Continent, as well as *R. rutilus* – confined to northern Europe, above the Alps.

DACE

Leuciscus leuciscus

The dashing habits of this tiny fish of the streams, flashing through the shallows, has given it the name 'dart'. Similar to the Roach (see p. 42-3), though slimmer and less colourful, the Dace does not attain the same mature size nor does it often choose to live in still waters.

Appearance Length 30 cm; weight 50 g. Greenish-black back, silvery sides shading to a creamy-white belly. Single fins are a muted grey; paired fins pale yellow with occasional reddish bloom. Anal and dorsal fins have pronounced concave appearance, which helps distinguish it from the immature chub (see p. 46-7).

Feeding Dace form large shoals when feeding. They eat insects, larvae, small crustaceans and algae. Young fish eat plankton.

Breeding Early spring during the hours of darkness in shallow, running water. At dawn, the breeding males drift downstream to deeper water to rest before continuing spawning. Gravid females stay close to the chosen gravel patches until they have shed all their eggs. These hatch in 2–3 weeks, depending on water temperature.

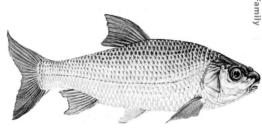

Dace are fast-maturing. Some may breed at a year old; most begin in their second year.

Distribution Widespread in England, but not often seen far north of the Scottish Border counties. Dace appear only locally in Ireland.

CHUB

Leusiscus cephalus

The Chub is a powerful, thickset fish, found in clean rivers and streams that offer a constant water flow over gravel or sandy bottoms. There are a few instances of still-water populations, particularly in East Anglia, where they have been introduced from adjacent streams.

Appearance 60 cm; weight 2 kg. Solid, round fish with a broad head, leading to the term 'loggerhead', though the head is not out of proportion to the body. Large mouth with no teeth. Like all Cyprinidae (carp family), it has only throat teeth (pharyngeals). Large silver scales, with a marked dark-banded edge and clearly defined lateral line. Upper body is deep purple-black, silver flanks fading to a creamy belly. Dorsal and anal fins have a convex edge (see Dace, p. 44); paired pelvic fins and anal fin are pale reddish.

Feeding Vegetable matter, small crustaceans and larvae. The Chub is one member of the carp family that predates on small fish fry, particularly just after spawning.

Breeding Chub breed in May. Like the Roach (see p.42-3), the males grow white breeding tubercles on the head and body. Sticky eggs are broadcast among waterweeds and gravels. Like most Cyprinidae, Chub will hybridise with other fish that choose similar spawning territory.

Distribution Widespread in England, the species does not appear north of the Scottish Border counties or in Ireland. Found right across Europe.

ORFE

Leusiscus idus

Also known as the Ide, this beautiful small carp was introduced from eastern Europe and Asia as a fish for garden ponds and aquariums. The golden variety is most popular, but escapes into a natural habitat tend to revert back to the normal, Rudd-like coloration. There are some breeding populations in rivers, ponds and small lakes.

Appearance Length 60 cm. See the Rudd (p. 52).

Feeding Larvae, minute crustaceans, and insects.

Breeding Breeds in early spring, choosing a stream with stony shallows.

GOLDFISH

Carassius auratus

The original ornamental Goldfish were brought to Britain from China in the early 17th century. Later introductions came from Portugal, where breeding stocks had become established after arriving from Asia. The higher water temperatures in that country have ensured the success of the Goldfish as a wild species. The same cannot be said in Britain, although Goldfish kept in shallow garden ponds will probably find sufficient heat to encourage them to spawn. Feeding, breeding and distribution are totally artificial; see Crucian Carp (p. 65) for the closest example.

Appearance Length 45 cm. Many colours and body shapes are known, but the wild fish resembles a Crucian Carp, though less deep-bodied.

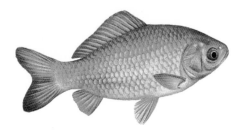

MINNOW

Phoxinus phoxinus

Minnows inhabit fast-flowing rivers and streams where, in the warmer months of the year, they can be seen as huge shoals, just under the water's surface. They prefer running water but will live in ponds that have clean water conditions. Indeed, the Minnow is an important indicator of water quality.

Appearance Length 12 cm; weight 100 g. Tiny, silver-brown body with vertical brown markings, sometimes confluent, along the flanks. Breeding males have a brilliant red-coloured belly and much darker head.

Feeding Fry eat minute planktonic food. Adults feed on algae and water insect larvae.

Breeding Begins in late May. Eggs are shed among loose gravel.

Distribution England, Wales, Ireland, southern Scotland and most of Europe.

GUDGEON

Gobio gobio

The Gudgeon is found in slow-flowing rivers, with clean, gravelly bottoms.

Appearance Length 20 cm; weight 40 g. Dull green-brown back, fading to a yellow belly; spots run along the upper body and lateral line. Fins are small and delicate, though the tail fin is large, muscular and forked.

Feeding Feeds on the riverbed, fry feeding on plankton, adults on larger insect larvae and crustaceans, for example freshwater shrimps (*Gammarus spp.*).

Breeding Spawns in May, shedding their sticky eggs among stones and waterweeds.

Distribution Throughout England and Ireland.

RUDD   *Scardinius erythrophthalmus*

One of nature's most beautiful fish, the Rudd species can be found in running waters, but only those where the flow is gentle, and in places that offer backwaters as an escape from the full force of spates. During the warm months of the year, Rudd are easily detected as they rise to take insects from the surface of the water. Like other members of the carp family, they form shoals, gathering in groups of the same age and body size.

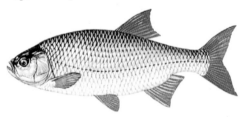

Appearance Length 41 cm; weight 1 kg. Flashing golden scales of a brilliant red hue, along the flanks and fins. Breeding males adopt brighter coloration and grow tubercles on their heads and bodies. To distinguish the Rudd from its near relative the Roach (pp.42-3), note that the bottom jaw is slightly longer than the bottom one, and the dorsal fin begins well behind the pelvic fins. Also, adult Rudd are much deeper than Roach of the same size.

Feeding Fry feed on minute organisms, adults eat water insects and their larvae, small crustaceans and some vegetable matter, plus the smallest fry of other species.

Breeding Begins in late May, or earlier, depending on water temperature. Shoals can be seen splashing and rolling among weeds where the eggs are deposited. Rudd hybridise with many other species, especially when there is competition for suitable spawning ground. Many thousands of eggs are produced and hatch in just over a week. The larvae attach themselves to vegetation for a few days.

Distribution Widespread throughout Europe, the Rudd prefers still-water habitats in England, Ireland, Wales and southern Scotland.

Roach x Rudd hybrid

TENCH

Tinca tinca

Not a species that one will see regularly, for it is demersal in habit and rarely rises to the upper water layers. It is a fish of lakes, ponds and slow-running rivers, having a strong preference for fertile waters with a lush growth of bottom weed. Like Carp (see p. 62), Tench can tolerate low oxygen levels, and they may be able to exist in a slightly saline water.

The Tench goes into a form of hibernation soon after the first of winter's early frosts, burying itself in the bottom mud. Occasional forays will be made in the spring on warm and sunny days, but it is not until May that this species begins to take a serious interest in group or shoal activity.

Appearance Length 70 cm; weight 3 kg. Unlike other carp family members, the Tench has a dark olive-green back, shading to rich golden flanks and an orange-yellow belly. Countless tiny scales, so small the fish can

Pelvic fins of male extend past the vent

look scaleless, liberally coated with the slime (traditionally believed to have healing powers). Small, reddish eyes and two barbules, one at each corner of the mouth. Fins are large, powerful and well rounded. Males have a thickened leading edge to their pelvic fins, which are also larger than those of the female.

Feeding Most water invertebrates, especially freshwater mussels and pond snails.

Breeding During June and July, depending on water temperature. Many sticky eggs are shed among soft waterweeds in shallow margins. They hatch quickly and the fry gather in large shoals to feed on algae and minute plankton. Growth is very slow and the species is renowned for its longevity.

Distribution Widespread throughout southern Europe and the British Isles, except most of Scandinavia, and Scotland above the Forth–Clyde valley.

BARBEL

Barbus barbus

This species is found in rivers that have a strong flow of water where, with its flattened belly, the Barbel is ideally suited to hugging the riverbed.

Appearance Length 102 cm; weight 4 kg. Bronze-green, elongated, muscular body, with clean, defined scales and a noticeable lateral line. Four pronounced barbules, two on the upper jaw and one in each corner of the mouth. Large and powerful fins, reddish at the junctions with the body. Dorsal fin has a serrated edge to the stiffened, leading ray. Breeding males have white tubercles.

Feeding Forages during the dark hours for tiny invertebrates, insect larvae and snails.

Breeding In early summer, among stones and loose gravel, after migrating to upstream shallows.

Distribution Introduced into the east midlands of England but widespread on the Continent, as far east as the Danube. Three closely related species live in Spain, northern Italy and the Balkans.

BLEAK

Alburnus alburnus

The Bleak forms huge shoals, swimming just under the surface in clean, slow-flowing rivers and streams where it forms the staple diet of many freshwater predators. There are still-water populations, but only as a result of introduction by fishermen. The scales of this tiny fish were once used to coat glass beads in the production of artificial pearls. Its breeding habits are unknown.

Appearance Length 20 cm. Small, slim fish with silvery scales.

Feeding Minute insect larvae and planktonic material near to the surface.

Distribution Throughout England and Europe.

BITTERLING   *Rhodeus sericeus amarus*

This is a small fish that lays its eggs in mussels.

Appearance Length 10 cm. Colourful, bronze-green body with a brilliant metallic stripe along the hind flanks – exaggerated in the male fish at spawning time.

Feeding Vegetation and minute creatures.

Breeding The female has a long ovipositor and deposits a few eggs in each open, freshwater mussel that she comes upon. The male fish ejects milt into the surrounding water; this is drawn into the mussel as it respirates. After hatching, about 18 days, the hatchlings leave the mussel having enjoyed a protected environment.

Distribution Continental Europe and localised introductions into England.

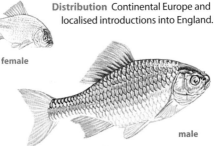

female

male

SILVER BREAM   *Blicca bjoerkna*

The Silver Bream is to be found in still waters and slow-moving rivers.

Appearance Length 35 cm. Delicate, small fish, lacking depth of colouring and size of the Common Bream (see p.60-1). Eyes are large and the single fins are muted grey, sometimes pinkish at the junction with the fish's body. Body very slimy and scales can be easily rubbed off.

Feeding Crustaceans, larvae and vegetation.

Breeding In June among weeds in muddy shallows; in Europe, it is known to hybridise with other bream species, such as the Common Bream.

Distribution Throughout Europe, confined to East Anglia in Britain, although it has been spreading, possibly with the help of fishermen.

COMMON BREAM   *Abramis brama*

A gregarious fish, the Common or Bronze Bream is
known as a still-water species but has a tolerance for
slow-flowing currents found in lowland, meandering
rivers. Common Bream form huge shoals that graze the
underwater vegetation like sheep, ever moving in their
quest for sufficient food. The presence of a shoal is
easily detected by the immense clouds of bubbles and
coloured water sent to the surface as the fish feed.

Appearance Length 80 cm; weight 5 kg. Silvery body
when young, resembling the Silver Bream (see p. 59). At
450 g, body darkens to deep brown, with bronzed
flanks and a creamy belly. Mature fish has a
pronounced hump, beginning behind the head,
curving up to the dorsal fin. Tail fin is markedly forked
and the anal fin long with a concave edge.

Feeding Feeds on the bottom of lakes and slow-
running rivers, eating larvae, crustaceans, worms.

Breeding During the hours of darkness in May in
shallows with lush weed growth. Spawning is noisy
with much splashing and rolling. The eggs are sticky,
adhering to the plant growth where they hatch in
about 14 days. The larvae remain attached to plants for
a period before starting to feed on plankton. Juvenile

growth is fast in warm waters, and the adult fish can attain huge weights, up to 9 kg.

Distribution Throughout Europe and the British Isles, though rarely north of the Scottish border.

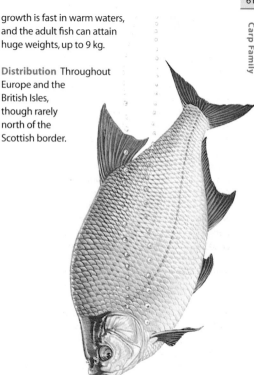

CARP

Cyprinus carpio

This species, the largest of the carp family (Cyprinidae), was introduced long ago to Britain and western Europe as a food source for humans. The Carp is native to the Far East where it has been successfully domesticated for centuries. Only the juvenile fish form shoals; adults, especially the huge specimens, adopt solitary behaviour. Carp favour well-weeded, still-

Common Carp

Mirror Carp

running rivers, lakes and ponds with deep water. There is a considerable tolerance to low oxygen levels, so even the smallest ponds can make a perfect home for this creature. Growth can be fast, particularly when the water is warm. Distribution is artificial.

Appearance Length 103 cm; weight 15–20 kg. Selective breeding has resulted in colour/scale aberrations. The wild fish or Common Carp is fully scaled; Mirror Carp have a few scales along the lateral line, and Leather Carp no scales. Common Carp have a purple back, shading to golden sides and cream underparts; the other two species are less colourful. All varieties have four barbules, two sprouting from the upper lip and one at each corner of the rubbery mouth. Fins are large and powerful.

Feeding Mature fish feed on larvae, invertebrates and crustaceans; fry feed on plankton.

Breeding During June among weeds in shallow areas. Many eggs are shed and hatch in a week or so. Larvae grow quickly, measuring over 10 cm long after a year. Adults attain sexual maturity in 3-5 years and can live 20 years or more.

Close-up of Carp's head showing barbels

CRUCIAN CARP *Carassius carassius*

Like the Common Carp (see p. 62), this species was introduced to Britain, probably from Germany, and prefers still waters and slow-flowing rivers. Distribution is artificial.

Appearance Length 40 cm; weight 750 g. Small, deep-bodied fish, readily identified by its lack of barbules and huge, sail-like, convex dorsal fin.

Feeding Larvae, minute crustaceans and plankton.

Breeding Breeds in summer and will hybridise with the larger Common Carp.

STONE LOACH
Noemacheilus

Loach are tiny nocturnal fish that live amongst stones, weedgrowth and debris at the bottom of small rivers and streams with a constant flow. Stone Loach show intolerance to the smallest amount of pollution.

Appearance Length 10 cm. Blotchy brown, often with a yellowy marbling. Dorsal and tail fins have dark spots in a patchwork pattern. Six barbules: four as a fringe to the upper lip and one at each corner of the mouth.

Feeding Bottom-dwelling invertebrates.

Breeding Spawns in late spring, setting adhesive eggs on to stones and gravel.

Distribution Throughout England and Ireland. This is a common species across Europe and into Asia.

SPINED LOACH *Cobitis taenia*

The Spined Loach is to be found in still waters and muddy, slow-running rivers. This scavenger fish is popular with aquarists.

Appearance Length 14 cm. Paler in ground colouring than the Stone Loach (see p. 66), blotching is less pronounced, with a row of dark spots extending from behind the gill case to the tail. Six barbules: four as a fringe to the upper lip and one at each corner of the mouth.

Feeding Minute organisms among river detritus.

Breeding Breeds in mid-spring, spreading eggs over plant roots and foliage.

Distribution Confined to eastern Britain, but widespread in Europe and Asia as far as Japan.

WELS

Silurus glanis

Introduced from Europe, the Wels or Catfish is a night-feeding fish that inhabits muddy lakes and slow-flowing rivers. Little is known about its breeding habits.

Appearance Length at least 150 cm; weight 12 kg. Black or dark bronze-grey in colour, and easily identified by its barbules: six on the head, two of which reach back beyond the pectoral fins.

Feeding Fish, amphibians and small swimming mammals.

Distribution Central and eastern Europe, where the species has grown to over 3 m.

BURBOT

Lota lota

A rarely seen member of the cod family (Gadidae), the Burbot may be observed at night, feeding in still waters and rivers. Its breeding habits are unknown.

Appearance Resembles the Ling (see p. 137).

Distribution Common on the Continent but confined to eastern England, some authorities considering it to be extinct.

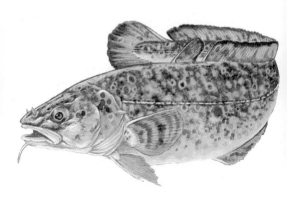

FRESHWATER EEL   *Anguilla anguilla*

Few fish have a more fascinating life story than the eel, which migrates for miles across the Atlantic Ocean. Both elvers and adult eels are said to migrate across land, between watercourses and enclosed still waters that have no connecting streams. It is distinctly possible, after periods of heavy rainfall, that there is sufficient moisture for the eels to wriggle across fields and even roads. Eel is a favourite dish in England, particularly the East End of London. Holland is a devoted eel country, specialising in smoked eel.

Appearance Length 51 cm (male), 142 cm (female); weight 2.5 kg. Newly hatched larvae are transparent; elvers have a muted, silver-grey appearance. Growing eels adopt a yellow colouring on the sides and belly.

Metamorphosis from egg to elver

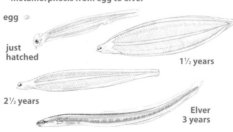

egg

just hatched

1½ years

2½ years

Elver 3 years

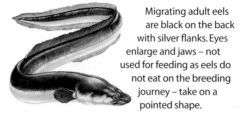

Migrating adult eels are black on the back with silver flanks. Eyes enlarge and jaws – not used for feeding as eels do not eat on the breeding journey – take on a pointed shape.

Feeding Mature and growing eels feed on larvae, crustaceans and the fry of other species. Adult eels also feed on dead animals.

Breeding Adults travel from Europe to the western Atlantic for spawning. After hatching, the larvae, or leptocephali, migrate back to Europe, carried for 3–4 years on warm ocean currents, during which they metamorphose into transparent, eel-shaped creatures (elvers) and ascend upriver. Some eels do not enter freshwater at all but stay within estuaries and saltwater inlets. An eel's length can indicate sexual maturity. At 60 cm, female fish begin moving downriver; males start their seaward journey when just over 40 cm long. Males spend 7–12 years feeding and growing in freshwater, and females 9–19 years.

Distribution The whole of western Europe and into the Mediterranean.

THREE-SPINED STICKLEBACK
Gasterosteus aculeatus

The Three-spined Stickleback is tolerant of saline conditions and can be found in estuaries and along shorelines.

Appearance Length 12 cm. A colourful fish, known to generations of small boys as the Redthroat. Breeding males adopt a bright red throat and belly.

Feeding Minute larvae and plankton.

Breeding Males build a nest and attract mature females to lay their eggs in this. The male then guards the eggs and tends the newly hatched fry.

Distribution Widespread in European waters and around the British Isles.

TEN-SPINED STICKLEBACK
Pungitius pungitius

The Ten-spined Stickleback spends its entire life in freshwater. It loves stagnant farm ponds and weed-choked streams but can be found in brackish waters.

Appearance Length 10 cm. Slightly smaller size than the Three-spined Stickleback (see p.72).

Feeding Minute larvae and plankton.

Breeding Males build a nest and attract mature females to lay their eggs in this. The male then guards the eggs and tends the newly hatched fry.

Distribution Widespread in European waters and around the British Isles.

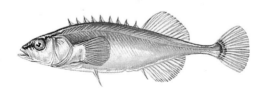

PERCH

Perca fluviatilis

The Perch is a predator and, like the Pike (see p. 38), regulates the number of fish contained in an area of water.

Appearance Length 51 cm; weight 2 kg. Purple-black back, green-gray flanks and a white belly. Underside fins are reddish. Highly recognisable are the vertical, dark bars on the sides and the two dorsal fins; the first has about 15 sharp spines with a black blotch on the rear end; the second, much smaller dorsal fin, has 15 or so soft, branched rays. Older fish have a deep, compressed body with a pronounced hump in front of the dorsal fins.

Feeding Tends to feed on small fry and does not appear to scavenge.

Breeding During May when the large breeding female fish are attended by a few smaller males. Many thousands of eggs are extruded as filamentous strands, woven among weed and sunken branches in shallow water. Easily seen, these are consumed in large quantities by waterfowl. But the Perch is a survivor; even stunted fish, with scarcely enough food, are capable of reproduction.

Distribution Widespread in most European countries, with the exception of northern Scotland and Norway.

ZANDER

Stizostedion lucioperca

Also known as the Pike-Perch, the species has taken the role of the Pike (see p. 38) as a population regulator in turbid waters. Conditions in drainage waters suit the lifestyle of the Zander, as it is tolerant of muddy water.

Appearance Length 130 cm; weight 3 kg. Sleek, silvery-green body with small scales, large fins and a forked tail. Dorsal fins are clearly divided. The anal fin also has two spines before the soft rays. A number of spots on the upper fins and tail. Teeth are sharp and those at the front of the mouth are long.

Feeding Totally predatory: fry eat larvae and tiny crustaceans. As they grow their diet changes to fish.

Breeding From May onwards when the water temperature is above 16°C, in waterweed and gravelly shallows. Eggs are laid on gravel bottom, then moved by the male fish into a nest which he guards.

Distribution Found in British rivers and drainage canals but not widespread. Originated in E and C Europe. It has since been introduced to Holland and France.

RUFFE

Gymnocephalus cernua

The Ruffe or Pope is a shoal fish of still waters and slow-running rivers, where it will be found in the deeper areas that are shaded from direct sunlight. Its breeding habits are unknown.

Appearance Length 15 cm. Small and looking much like a juvenile Perch (see p. 74-5) except that the eyes are large and purple. Green-black back, shading through grey-green to an off-white belly. Fins are large and the dorsal fins, spined at the forepart, are joined.

Feeding Smaller invertebrates, young amphibians and insect larvae.

Distribution Throughout Europe and eastern England.

LARGE-MOUTHED BLACK BASS
Micropteras salmoides

Similar to the Small-mouthed Black Bass, *Micropterus dolomieu*, also part of this N American genus forming part of the sunfish family. Has been successfully introduced in Europe, where it has spread through many waters as a result of its sportfishing potential.

Appearance Length 83 cm; weight 2.5 kg. Bronze-green body, with a few dark bars on the sides and gill case. Spined and soft-rayed dorsal fins are joined with a pronounced dip between them.

Feeding Smaller fish species, invertebrates and insects.

Breeding The male fish excavates a nest in the bed of a lake or pond. He encourages the female to lay her eggs and then guards the eggs and emergent young.

Distribution Throughout France, Continental N Europe and localised areas of southern England.

PUMPKINSEED

Lepomis gibbosus

Sunfish Family

Introduced from North America into Europe, this small colourful fish is to be found in weeded still waters and slow-running streams; it has a tolerance for shallow, warm conditions. The Pumpkinseed has been put into a few English waters as the species is a prolific breeder.

Appearance Length 22 cm. Highly coloured, deep-bodied fish with joined dorsal fins. Originally an aquarium pet.

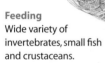

Feeding Wide variety of invertebrates, small fish and crustaceans.

Breeding In spring males build nests among waterweeds, where they guard eggs and young until ready to depart the nest.

Distribution Originating in North America, has been successfully spread throughout western Europe. Not widespread in England.

BULLHEAD

Cottus gobio

A shy, nocturnal species, the Bullhead or Miller's Thumb lives among stones and thick waterweeds.

Appearance Length 15 cm. Brown-marbed body; head and forepart of the body having a flattened appearance. Fins are large with a division between the two dorsals. There is a spine on the top of the gill cases.

Feeding Minute creatures and invertebrates.

Breeding During the spring. The male guards the eggs, which are laid in a nest scraped out from among the fine gravels.

Distribution Europe, Scandinavia and England.

COMMON GOBY *Pomatoschistus microps*

A small shoalfish found in fresh, slow-flowing waters, as well as river mouths, estuaries and around the coast in the littoral zone. It is the only member of the goby group of fish that will enter freshwater.

Appearance Length 6 cm. Dorsal fins, the first of which is spined, are separated and the pelvic fins are fused together to form a weak sucking pad, with which it can adhere to stones.

Feeding Invertebrates, small fry and plankton.

Breeding The male fish guards the eggs after spawning, which may happen several times in a season.

Distribution Northern Europe, down to Spain.

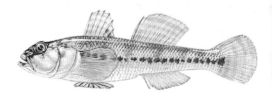

THE MARINE ENVIRONMENT

Looking out from the shoreline, we can divide the sea into three zones: the splash zone, the littoral zone, and the continental shelf. Each zone has a depth significance as a fish habitat (see diagram opposite).

Some fish are described as pelagic, or surface-dwelling. Demersal species are those that choose to live and feed on or close to the seabed. Between these two extremes there are countless habitats and the necessary fishlife to fill them.

An example of fish finding their own level is an offshore reef, which rises out of deep water to within a few feet of the surface. Feeding over the tip of the reef will be pelagic fish. Midwater species will be living down in the rock crevices. Swimming at the reef base will be the true demersal species. One cannot say with accuracy where a particular species ought to be found, other than to suggest that certain families of fish will occupy well-defined locations of depth and light. There must always be some overlap, especially when we consider juvenile fish, which have yet to occupy an adult niche in the ecosystem.

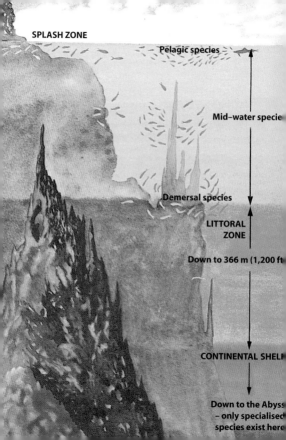

SPLASH ZONE

Pelagic species

Mid–water specie

Mid–water specie

Demersal species

LITTORAL ZONE

Down to 366 m (1,200 ft

CONTINENTAL SHEL

Down to the Abyss
– only specialised
species exist here

Shark Family

PORBEAGLE SHARK *Lamna nasus*

The Porbeagle prefers cold, clean and deep ocean water and is rarely found in shallow, sandy or muddy waters. The species is fond of establishing its own territory, especially over offshore reefs.

Appearance Length 300 cm. Portly, almost cylindrical body, with dark blue-black upper parts, shading to a dirty white belly. Fins are large and powerful, giving incredible speed through the water. Two horizontal 'keels' at the junction of the tapering body and tail fin. Upper lobe of the tail is largest, with a notch near the tip. Eyes noticeably large, enabling the shark to hunt over murky, weeded ground rather than nearer the ocean surface. Teeth sharp and wedge-shaped, with a small 'cusp' or ridge on either side of each tooth.

Feeding Follows Herring and Mackerel shoals. When resident in a rocky environment, feeds on Pollack.

Breeding Ovoviviparous – giving birth to 2–4 pups, each about 45 cm in length.

Distribution Found throughout the Northern Hemisphere at most times of year; in Britain, mainly off the western shores.

Detail of teeth

MAKO SHARK

Isurus oxyrinchus

This is an oceanic, pelagic fish that migrates to North Atlantic waters in high summer. The Mako is a larger-growing species than the Porbeagle (see p. 84-5), with a far wider distribution.

Appearance Length 350 cm. Sleek in shape, with a deep blue upper body shading quickly to pure white underparts. Unlike the Porbeagle, only one horizontal keel and no basal cusps on the sharply pointed teeth.

Feeding Live fish of any species.

Breeding See Porbeagle Shark. Being larger than Porbeagles, Makos give birth to more pups.

Distribution Worldwide.

Detail of teeth

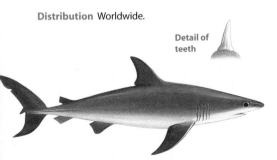

THRESHER SHARK *Alopias vulpinus*

The Thresher Shark, with its characteristic tail fin, is an infrequent inshore visitor except in certain localised habitats. It would seem that we only see the smaller specimens of this species in Britain. In tropical waters, the Thresher Shark can be as heavy as one ton (1,016 kg)!

Appearance Length 460 cm. Highly recognisable because of its gigantic, scythe-like tail fin. A drab, dark grey on the back, shading to off-white flanks and belly.

Feeding Pelagic shark often seen on the surface harrying shoals of Pilchards and Mackerel where it 'rounds up' the baitfish by thrashing its tail and rapidly circling them.

Breeding Ovoviviparous – producing one or two live young each breeding season.

Distribution Visits the North Atlantic area during the summer, travelling as far north as the Norwegian coast.

BASKING SHARK *Cetorhinus maximus*

A huge, harmless fish of the upper water layers, it is often seen by holiday-makers as it slowly patrols the coastal current line in high summer. It usually congregates in family groups.

Appearance Can attain a huge size: length up to 900 cm, weight over 3 tons (3,048 kg). Some variation in colouring. Adults usually dark brown with lighter flanks; juveniles have a softer, muted back and fawn flanks and belly. Light blotches of colour possible on fish of all ages. Highly recognisable are five enormous gill slits that begin on the top of the back and extend to just under the throat.

Feeding Plankton, but can attain a huge weight on this minute food.

Breeding Viviparous. Gestation period is thought to be in excess of two years, when only one or two infants are produced, thought to be in excess of 150 cm each. Evidence of some parental care: pups are seen in constant contact with a particular adult.

Distribution Both sides of the North Atlantic Ocean, up to the Arctic.

HAMMERHEAD SHARK
Sphyrna zygaena

The Hammerhead Shark, with its distinctive head shape, is a frequent visitor to Britain from more southerly, warmer climes, where there are a number of closely related species.

Appearance Length 400 cm. Sleek, streamlined body that can grow to over 5 m long. Small head with eyes located on the outer extremity of a flattened oblong. Nostrils are on the corners of the head, just in front of the eyes. Smaller mouth than other species of similar size.

Feeding Fish, especially sting rays.

Breeding Ovoviviparous – producing about 30 pups at each breeding season. Gravid females have been caught, commercially, at most periods in a year. Length of gestation unknown.

Distribution In warmer seas, though visiting British waters in high summer.

BLUE SHARK

Prionace glauca

The most common of our summer shark visitors, it arrives off the coast of Cornwall in late June.

Appearance Length 400 cm. Slim body; deep, rich blue on the back, lightening to azure on the flanks, fading to a snow-white belly. Large pectoral fins.

Feeding Pelagic feeder, following shoals of mackerel, pilchards and sardines on the warm currents that press northward from the tropical region.

Breeding Viviparous – a large litter of pups, perhaps up to 40, is expelled, their size and number depending on the length and maturity of the mother.

Distribution Western coasts of the British Isles, France, Spain and Portugal. During exceptionally warm summers it will migrate as far north as Norway.

SMOOTHHOUND *Mustelus mustelus*

This is a slow-moving, demersal species with crushing jaws ideally suited for a diet of crustaceans.

Appearance Length 150 cm. Grey in coloration, fading to white. Thickset with large fins, lacking spots on the body.

Feeding Crabs, lobsters, prawns and small fish.

Breeding Viviparous – producing up to 20 young.

Distribution North Atlantic.

STARRY SMOOTHOUND
Mustelus asterias

This species is closely related to the Smoothound
Mustelus mustelus (see p. 92).

Appearance Length 140 cm. Similar in shape to
Mustelus mustelus, with a heavy sprinkling of white
spots across the back and flanks.

Feeding Crabs, lobsters, prawns and small fish.

Breeding Ovovivaparous, but little further is known.

Distribution North Atlantic.

SPURDOG

Squalus acanthias

The most common of the small sharks to inhabit British waters, Spurdog travel in huge, predatory shoals. This shark prefers the deeper ocean, not shallow, muddy waters. It makes a large contribution to the wet fish trade. Thousands of tons are fished each year and the boneless flesh is sold as 'Rock Eel'.

Appearance Length 90 cm (male); 120 cm (female). Streamlined, pale grey body, with a few lighter spots along the sides. No anal fin. Each of the dorsal fins has a sharp spine at its leading edge. Believed to be venomous, this can inflict a painful wound, often requiring medical attention.

Feeding Predatory, feeding on smaller fish.

Breeding Ovoviviparous – up to a dozen pups each breeding season.

Distribution Throughout the North Atlantic.

BULL HUSS

Scyliorhinus stellaris

This small shark is often described as the Greater-spotted Dogfish or Nursehound. Similar to the Roughhound (see p.96), it is less widespread and plentiful. Demersal in habit, it patrols a rougher, more stony seabed for food.

Appearance Length 160 cm. Striking colouring, almost black on the back; flanks are fawn, blotched with an uneven dark brown pattern.

Feeding Crustaceans and small fish.

Breeding Thought to take place in spring. Eggs are contained in a rectangular capsule or 'purse' the colour of brown seaweed. At each corner is a spiralled tendril which is used to attach the egg cases to kelp and weeds. The young are several centimetres long when they emerge from the capsules after a growing period of many months.

Distribution S British waters and the European coast.

ROUGHOUND   *Scyliorhinus caniculus*

Much smaller than the Bull Huss (see p. 95), this fish, also known as the Lesser-spotted Dogfish, is given the name Roughound because of its abrasive skin texture. When picked up the fish has a nasty habit of wrapping itself around an arm, which can tear skin off! Unlike the Bull Huss, this nocturnal, bottom-dwelling little scavenger tends to avoid rough ground, preferring to scour the open sands, muddy estuaries and weeded shallows for food.

Appearance Length 100 cm. Less colourful than the Bull Huss, having a mass of dark brown blotches over its brown body.

Feeding Fish, crustaceans. Vast shoals of Roughound quickly remove all small fish from a habitat.

Breeding Egg-laying like the Bull Huss, although the capsules are much smaller in size.

Distribution Similar to Bull Huss but more widespread (and more numerous).

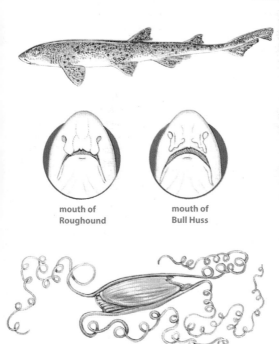

mouth of
Roughound

mouth of
Bull Huss

egg case of Dogfish

TOPE

Galeorhinus galeus

A small, fast-swimming shark that haunts the inshore, shallow waters of the British Isles and European seaboard. It is fairly widespread in distribution and there are related species around the world. Locally, it has become a source of food for humans. The fish's skin, when cured, is extremely tough and has been used as a form of leather; it is also used as a smoothing material for cabinet-makers and other woodworkers.

Appearance Length 200 cm. Slender, brown-grey body, with smallish fins and a distinctive, deeply notched tail. Head has a flattened shape, when viewed from above. Eyes are quite large with a nictitating membrane moving from the front to the rear of each eye. Sharp teeth with a serrated edge at the back. A female fish of 75 lb (34 kg) was landed at Tenby, South Wales some years ago; male Tope rarely exceed 30 lb (13.6 kg) in weight.

Feeding Demersal, feeding on the smaller shoal species and flatfish of inshore areas. Species is known to hunt in a pack when mackerel are plentiful.

Breeding Viviparous, breeding in summer when they produce about 30 pups, though small females expel considerably fewer offspring. It is interesting to note that the large fish that swim into inshore waters are usually gravid females searching for their young. No male fish accompanying the females at this time, possibly because females view the males as predators on the pups.

Distribution Sandy bays and inlets as found on the South Wales coast, Cardigan Bay, Thames Estuary, the Wash, Morecombe Bay, Solway Firth and a number of well-known sea areas in Ireland.

SKATES AND RAYS

The body of all skates and rays is compressed, giving them a flattened shape. This distinctive appearance has given rise to confusion over what a flatfish is. Basically, flatfish – such as Plaice and Flounder – are compressed sideways and they swim on their sides. The dark body colour and eyes are on one side of the fish, to the right or left. (See Flatfish: Left- and Right-handedness, pp. 196–7). Skates and rays are compressed from spine to belly through their bodies and swim with their bellies to the seabed. Body coloration is on the upper side, as are the eyes and spiracles.

There is no biological difference between skates and rays. The anatomical differences can be simply defined as skates having long noses and a distinctive diamond shape, whereas rays have short noses and a more circular body shape. Skate grow much larger than any of the rays.

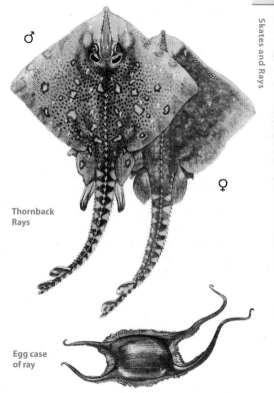

♂

♀

Thornback
Rays

Egg case
of ray

THORNBACK RAY

Raja clavata

The Thornback Ray is a widespread species that favours inshore waters of shallow depth. It can be found on storm beaches in a few feet of water, although the 9–18 m line is a more certain depth.

Appearance Length 100 cm; weight 15 kg. Wide variation in colouring, though a drab grey-brown is usual, and a number of darker blotches or spots may be present. More angular than other rays with a pronounced wave to the leading edge of the wings. Two small dorsal fins far back on the tail. Spines are in a single row running along the spine and tail, flanked by secondary rows at either side of the tail. There may be a patch of spines towards the extremity of each wing and, sometimes, a smaller patch on the underside of the wings. See p.101 for illustration.

Feeding Rays' crushing teeth are ideal for feeding on crustaceans, but they eat almost anything – for example, small fish, prawns and worms buried in mud.

Breeding Like all rays and skates, it is fertilised internally and the resulting eggs are expelled in leathery, brown capsules called 'mermaid's purses'.

Distribution European coastal shallows.

BLONDE RAY

Raja brachyura

A locally common ray of southern and western sea areas, the species is usually found in depths of about 37 m, but immature specimens will feed almost up to the tideline. See Thornback Ray (p. 102) for Feeding, Breeding and Distribution.

Appearance Length 100 cm; weight 15 kg. Body covered with small dark brown spots on a light brown ground. These spots extend to the extreme margins of the wings. On adult fish the upper, coloured body is often liberally dotted with fine spines. Few thorns are present, confined to the tail.

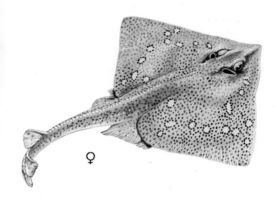

♀

SPOTTED RAY

Raja montagui

Although closely resembling the Thornback and Blonde Ray (see pp. 102–3), the Spotted or Homelyn Ray does not attain the size of either species. See Thornback Ray for Feeding, Breeding and Distribution.

Appearance Length 80 cm; weight rarely exceeds 3.5 kg. Larger speckles of dark colour than Thornback or Blonde Ray, and these do not extend out to the wing margins. Some adults have an ocellus, a circular patch surrounded by dark spots, on the wings. Spines along the spinal ridge and on the inner leading edge of the wings and a few irregular thorns on the body.

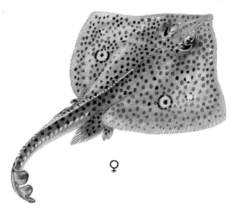

♀

STARRY RAY

Raja radiata

This species favours slightly deeper water than other rays. It is a prolific fish that forms a major part of trawled catches. See Thornback Ray (p. 102) for Breeding.

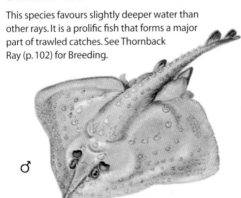

Appearance Length 60–90 cm. Creamy-brown in body colour with a smattering of light patches and black spots; rough upper surface covered in sharp spines. Clearly defined line of large curved thorns running from behind the eyes back to the dorsal fins.

Feeding Like most rays, feeds on crustaceans but live fish are also taken.

Distribution More northerly distribution than other rays – up to the Shetland Isles.

CUCKOO RAY

Raja naevus

This is a fairly common ray, found in depths of 18.3 m and over. See Thornback Ray (p. 102) for Feeding and Breeding.

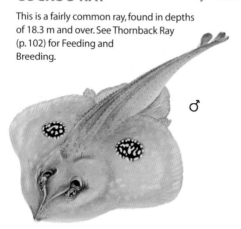

♂

Appearance Length 70 cm; weight does not exceed 2.3 kg. Easily identifiable by two circular yellow and black ocelli, lying on a body ground colour of pale brown. No large thorns, only patches of small spines on the upper surface and two rows of thicker spines along each side of the tail.

Distribution Around the British Isles, down to the Mediterranean.

SANDY RAY

Raja circularis

This larger-growing species of ray is found in deep, offshore waters. Little is known of the lifestyle of this fish, although many Sandy Rays are brought ashore as part of commercial boat catches. See Thornback Ray (p. 102) for Feeding and Breeding.

Appearance Length 120 cm; weight 5 kg. Rich brown in colour with a number of perfectly symmetrical light spots on the wings. Upper surface has patches of fine spines; two rows of stout, curved spines either side of the tail. No median line thorns present.

Distribution Northern and western distribution.

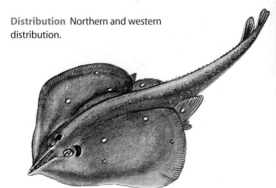

SMALL-EYED RAY *Raja microocellata*

The Small-eyed Ray is so called because the fish's eyes are much smaller than in other species. See Thornback Ray (p. 102) for Feeding and Breeding.

Appearance Length 80 cm; weight 6 kg. Relatively small in size, also called 'Painted Ray' because of the mass of light, wavy marblings on a pale cream or yellowy background. Spines are grouped closely along the tail, towards the snout.

Distribution Southerly in distribution, rarely found north of south-west England, and southern Ireland.

UNDULATE RAY

Raja undulata

Like the Small-eyed Ray (p. 108), this fish is found in similar sandy seabed habitats with a similar distribution. See Thornback Ray (p. 102) for Feeding and Breeding.

Appearance Length 100 cm; weight 7 kg. Like Small-eyed Ray, species is relatively small and with waving patterns of colour but in 'negative' form – dark chocolate brown, with white spotted edgings, on a mid-brown body.

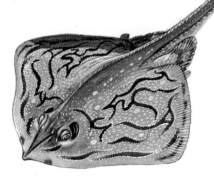

TORPEDO RAY

Torpedo nobiliana

The Torpedo Ray is an uncommon summer visitor to our shores. It has the reputation of delivering a high voltage

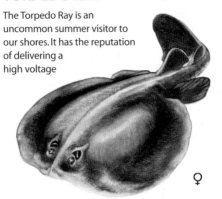

♀

electric shock if handled. It may be that the fish uses this weapon to stun its live fish prey or as a security against attack by larger predators! Little is known about its feeding and breeding habits.

Appearance Length 180 cm. Body is round, dark or muddy blue, with large pelvic, dorsal and tail fins. No sharp thorns or spines.

Distribution Southern and western inshore waters of the British Isles and French coast.

STING RAY

Dasyatis pastinaca

Sting Rays are often found in the warmer months, lying in shallow water or around offshore sandbanks. Like the Torpedo Ray (see p. 110), this is another dangerous member of the ray family. The wound caused by the sting is painful and can cause severe discomfort or even death. Little is known about its feeding and breeding habits.

Appearance Width 60 cm; weight 30 kg. Single, serrated stinging spine grows from the upper surface of the whip-like tail. Occasionally more than one of these spines can be seen growing from a common root position.

Distribution Often found off North Sea sandbanks and into East Anglian estuaries.

♂

COMMON SKATE

Raja batis

The Common or Grey Skate lives in deep water of 30–270 m. A fairly common fish, this skate achieves a large body size and weight but is only second in size to the White Skate (see p. 114).

Appearance Length 210 cm; weight 90 kg. Dirty grey or brown on the upper surface occasionally with marbling of lighter and darker patches of colour. Belly is never white but has a pale grey background, liberally dotted with darker blotches and spots. Immature specimens have no spines or noticeable thorns. Adults have at least one row, possibly more, of hard thorns along the spinal ridge and tail back to the dorsal fins. Male adults, distinguished by their claspers, have spines over the upper disc area; females only have spines around the head and leading edge of the wings. Spines under the snout in both sexes.

Feeding Demersal, feeding on crustaceans and small fish on or close to the seabed. Traps its prey by flopping its huge wings down over the creature while manoeuvring the prey towards its mouth.

Breeding Skates are fertilised internally and the female ejects a number of leathery capsules containing the egg. Thought to breed through summer and autumn. Depending on temperature, eggs hatch in four months or so.

Distribution Widespread in the north Atlantic Ocean from Iceland south to Portugal.

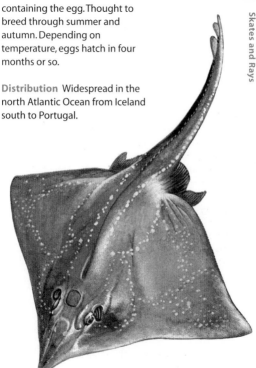

WHITE SKATE

Raja alba

This species frequents more southerly waters than the Common Skate and is the largest growing of the three indigenous species (see Common and Long-nosed Skate, p.112 and p.115). See Common Skate for Feeding and Breeding.

Appearance Length can exceed 300 cm; weight can be over 250 kg. More pointed snout than other species, often described as bottle-nosed, and the leading edge of the wings has a convex bulge. Easily identified by its pure white underside.

Distribution Found regularly off the Atlantic coast of Ireland.

♀

LONG-NOSED SKATE *Raja oxyrhynchus*

The smallest and least common of our three skates (see Common and White Skate, pp. 112-114), its lifestyle is similar to the Common Skate and it is found in the same environments, although adult fish appear to have a liking for deeper water. See Common Skate for Feeding and Breeding.

Appearance Length 125 cm; weight 40 kg. Easily identified by exceptionally elongated snout and deeply concave leading edge to the wings. Dorsal colour is dark brown-grey, with light and dark brown marbling; belly varies from dirty grey to almost black with patches of black spots or streak marks.

Distribution Similar to Common Skate but less widespread and not as far north as Iceland.

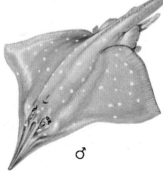

♂

SPRAT

Sprattus sprattus

The Sprat is a pelagic species that closely resembles the Herring but is much smaller and deeper in the body when adult.

Appearance Length 18 cm. Identified by saw-edged belly and position of the pelvic fins, which originate in front of the leading edge of the dorsal fin. Silver scaled, with a greenish tinge on the back.

Feeding Feed on plankton and minute fish fry.

Breeding Due to the many different races among the Herring population, spawning takes place at different times of the year. Lower North Sea fish spawn in early spring.

Distribution Widespread over the eastern Atlantic.

HERRING
Clupea harengus

This fish is one of the most important food species to humans. Under enormous commercial fishing pressures, the Herring manages to survive in huge shoals across the whole of the North Atlantic. There are several associated species in other parts of the world. The Herring shows a remarkable tolerance towards waters of low salinity, such as estuaries, and it engages in long migrations annually to seek food and to spawn.

Appearance Length 40 cm; weight 450 g. A greenish tinge to scales on the back, fading to silver on the flanks.

Feeding Pelagic, feeding on plankton and minute fish fry.

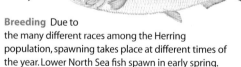

Breeding Due to the many different races among the Herring population, spawning takes place at different times of the year. Lower North Sea fish spawn in early spring.

Distribution Throughout the North Atlantic, where warm currents from the North Atlantic Drift meet arctic water.

PILCHARD

Sardina pilchardus

Looking very like a Herring (see p. 117), the Pilchard is another valuable food fish, both fresh and canned. Indeed, it replaces herring as a food fish in temperate and sub-tropical waters. When immature, they are called sardines.

Appearance Length 28 cm; weight 250 g. Two distinct features distinguish it from the Herring: radiating streaks on each gill case, and a rounded belly.

Feeding Pelagic, feeding exclusively on plankton.

Breeding Spawning through all the summer months in southern British waters and the whole year through in the Mediterranean.

Distribution Southerly distribution, ranging from the Mediterranean up to the English Channel and western coasts of Ireland.

ANCHOVY

Engraulis encrasicolus

At one time the Anchovy was known to shoal in vast numbers in the Ijsselmeer (Zuyder Zee) before barrages were erected to prevent the ingress of saltwater. See Pilchard (p. 118) for Feeding, and Herring (p. 117) for Breeding.

Appearance Length 20 cm; 150 g. Small, silvery body; mouth is a different shape, a more horizontal slit than seen in other herring-type fishes.

Distribution Southerly distribution. Found in temperate waters off the European coast, through the Mediterranean and into the Sea of Azov.

GARFISH

Belone belone

Like the Mackerel (see p. 148-9) and often seen in its company, Garfish are extremely fast swimmers, renowned for leaping clear of the water. The species has green bones, which causes it to be viewed with suspicion as a table fish, although the flesh is succulent.

Appearance Length 94 cm; weight 350 g. Streamlined, slender body, built for speed; green upper body shading to a creamy belly. Easily identified by its elongated beak, full of sharp teeth. Scales are tiny and the lateral line is positioned rather low on the body.

Feeding Pelagic feeder, harrying shoals of fry that swim just under the surface.

Breeding Spawns April–June. Eggs, which have long filaments that attach to rocks and gravels, hatch in about six weeks.

Distribution Widespread in the eastern Atlantic, visiting inshore waters in high summer.

SKIPPER
Scomberesox saurus

The Skipper or Saury Pike resembles a Garfish (p. 120) and is a summer visitor from warmer waters. Its common name is derived from its habit of skipping, lightly, out of the water to clear obstacles or escape from predators. See Garfish for Feeding.

Appearance Length 46 cm. Can be distinguished from a garfish by looking at the beak and fins. The skipper's beak is much shorter, relative to the length of the body. Its underjaw is slightly longer than the upper part of the beak. Both jaws contain a series of very small teeth. Anal and dorsal fins have an anterior section made up of finned rays, with the remaining parts formed as small finlets.

Breeding A pelagic spawning species, releasing eggs when water temperature is correct.

Distribution Similar in distribution to the Garfish and Mackerel (see p. 148), with whom it is found.

CONGER EEL

Conger conger

The Conger Eel is a fish that people love to hate. This may be caused by its snake-like appearance or because of its fixed, almost hypnotising stare; it is definitely a species that deserves to be handled carefully. The mouth is full of very sharp teeth and a Conger Eel can live out of water for an extended period, biting long after it appears dead! The species has a similar life history to the Freshwater Eel (see p. 70) in that it undertakes a once-in–a-lifetime journey, over vast distances, to the breeding ground.

This nocturnal-feeding eel lives in dark holes and among rocks and weeds, ideal ambush points for what is a demersal and fairly slow-moving species. Harbour walls provide cracks and crevices for the Conger to occupy, particularly if there are working fishing boats using the port. The attraction is waste fish falling into the water. Larger eels live offshore in deep water, where wrecks and reefs are a favoured habitat, providing a 'larder' of live fodder fish. Immature Conger Eels appear to favour shallow, inshore environments.

Appearance Length 305 cm; weight can exceed 45 kg. Coloration depends on habitat. Over open ground, with few weeded rocks, has a grey back and almost white belly. Living in wrecks and on reefs, may be nearly totally black. Dorsal fin extends from behind the head to the tip of the tail. Anal fin is much shorter and begins close behind the vent.

Feeding Baby Conger Eels feed on small crustaceans. Adults feed on larger prey – lobsters, edible crabs and live fish.

Breeding During summer in deep waters near to Madeira, spawns in mid-water and dies. After hatching, the larvae drift on warm ocean currents north-east to the European shores. Journey takes 2–3 years, and during the latter part the tiny creatures undergo a metamorphic change (see Freshwater Eel, p. 70), completed as they arrive in littoral waters.

Distribution Rocky coasts of the eastern and western Atlantic; into the Mediterranean and down to the equator.

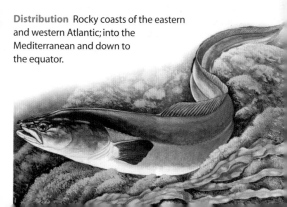

PIPEFISH

Sygnathus and *Neophis*

There are six species of pipefish, which can be found standing upright among eelgrass and other seaweeds. The genus *Syngnathus* has three species: *S. typhle*, the Broad-nosed Pipefish; *S. acus*, the Great Pipefish; and *S. rostellatus*, Nilsson's Pipefish. There are two species within the genus *Neophis*: *N. lumbriciformis*, the Worm Pipefish and *N. ophidion*, the Straight-nosed Pipefish. One other species remains, *Entelurus aequoreus*, the Snake Pipefish, which is oceanic in habit and relatively uncommon in shallow water. All pipefish are similar in appearance and generally 30–50 cm in length.

Feeding Minute shrimps, fish fry and planktonic animals.

Breeding Most significant characteristic of all pipefish is that the male incubates the eggs. He gathers the eggs after the female has expelled them; these are either contained in a pouch under the belly, or adhere to the abdomen of the male parent. Males within the genus *Syngnathus* keep both the fertilised eggs and hatching young in their pouches until the fry are about 2 cm.

Distribution Littoral waters of European coasts.

COD

Gadus morhua

The Cod ranks first among the world's food fish. Sadly, predation by commercial fishers has greatly reduced cod populations. It is a shoal fish, living over the continental shelf and in the shallow coastal waters but making long migrations in search of food and at spawning time. Demersal in habit, the species will frequently leave the seabed to predate among herring and sprat shoals. In winter, when sprats are shoaled up near to the coastline, large groups of cod will swim in very shallow water following their prey.

Appearance Length 190 cm. Highest recorded weight in America over 90.7 kg; average weight for European fish 4.5–18.1 kg. Widely varying coloration depending largely on environment: remarkable yellow marbled pelage speckled with brown streaks when migratory; red or dark brown colouring when the non-migrating fish is immature and living among inshore rocks and weedbeds. Both colour forms have a defined broad white lateral line, gently curving over the pectoral fins. Three dorsal fins and two anal fins. Large head; almost one-third the body length in adults. In old and spawning fish the belly sags, giving the underparts a dropsied appearance. Elongated barbule below the chin; upper jaw extends well beyond the lower. Lips thick and rubbery.

Feeding A scavenger, the Cod's diet includes almost anything edible and a lot of things that are not, even bottles and stones (probably swallowed because of a sea anemone or shellfish attached to them). Crustaceans form a large part of the food, as well as molluscs, echinoderms and sometimes fish. Inshore, it feeds over marine worm beds.

Breeding Prolific spawner, expelling millions of eggs. These are pelagic; hatching time varies with ambient temperature but 12 days is the average for British waters. After a few months spent feeding on plankton in the upper layers, the larvae swim to the bottom to begin their demersal life.

Distribution Widespread in arctic and temperate waters on both sides of the Atlantic Ocean.

HADDOCK   *Melanogrammus aeglefinus*

At one time the Haddock was almost as important to commercial fisheries as the Cod (see p. 126-7), but humankind's appetite for this fish has ensured the demise of former huge shoals. Usually found near to the sea floor, often in schools.

Appearance Length 112 cm; weight rarely exceeds 4.5 kg. However, growth rates differ depending on the area, and females often grow faster than males. Blue-brown back with silvery flanks and a black, curved lateral line. Elongated upper jaw with a barbule below the chin. Black blotch just above the pectoral fins, distinguishing it from Cod, and is said to be a fingerprint of the fisherman, St Peter. First dorsal is sharply pointed, tail deeply forked.

Breeding Spawns from winter to late spring after migrating into deep water. Following the protracted breeding period, March to late June, returns to shallow inshore waters. Eggs (around 300,000) hatch within one to three weeks at 4–10°C. Juveniles spend a longer time in the upper part of the sea after metamorphosis than Cod. They become demersal after their first few months and mature at 3–5 years. They usually do not move far from the spawning ground.

Feeding Demersal in habit, forms into travelling shoals that favour feeding over soft seabeds where there are colonies of shellfish and crustaceans – scallops, mussels, prawns and small crabs – as well as worms and sandeels.

Distribution Widespread in the North Atlantic from the Arctic Circle down to the north Portugese coast. Found throughout UK waters, but most likely to be found in the North Sea.

POUTING

Trisopterus luscus

A widely distributed small cod, this species inhabits rough ground, reefs and wrecks. It has little commercial value.

Appearance Length 45 cm; weight 2 kg. Small, deep-bodied, with a bronze ground colour, dark brown back and vertical bars of darker shading. Pelvic fins and first dorsal are long and sharply pointed; tail square-cut. Large eyes and a long barbule give this fish the common name of Bib. Distinct dark blotch at the base of the pectoral fin.

Feeding Shrimps, small crabs and tiny fish.

Breeding Breeds in the spring. Little else is known.

Distribution Warmer sea areas of Britain and the Bay of Biscay.

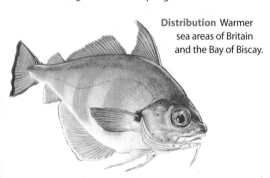

WHITING
Merlangius merlangus

This species swims in huge, predatory shoals over soft seabeds. Although not the most popular food fish, it is an important food species.

Appearance Length 70 cm; weight 2 kg. Slender, silvery body with no barbule (unlike most of the other cod family members). Mass of spiky teeth, used to grasp live prey. Anal fin longer than in the Pouting (see p. 130); pelvic fins elongated, possibly acting as organs of touch.

Feeding Small fish and crustaceans.

Breeding Matures in its third year and spawns in the spring. After hatching, the fry, which live in the pelagic layer, are spread over vast distances by the ocean currents.

Distribution Widespread over the North Atlantic from the Arctic Circle down to the Mediterranean.

POLLACK

Pollachius pollachius

Prefer to haunt offshore reefs and areas of broken ground, striking from ambush points among thick kelp.

Appearance Length 130 cm. Splendid coloration: red-brown back shading to golden flanks. Distinctive dark lateral line, like a strand of twisted thread, curving over the pectoral fins. Lower jaw considerably longer than the upper and there is no barbule.

Feeding Predates on small fish in the depths during daylight hours. As darkness falls, zooplankton and small fry rise to the surface, which the Pollack follow closely to feed on.

Breeding Spawns in early spring. The young favour inshore waters where they feed on minute creatures and the fry of many species.

Distribution Eastern side of the Atlantic, around the British Isles, chiefly in western areas of clear water, and from Norway to Morocco.

COALFISH

Pollachius virens

The Coalfish is similar to the Pollack (see p. 132).

Appearance Length 130 cm; weight 12.5 kg. More rounded in shape than the Pollack and jaws almost equal in length. White, straight lateral line identifies it best from the Pollack. Body ground colour rich black, with a definite greenish sheen. Rudimentary barbule hardly discernible in adult fish.

Feeding Almost entirely predatory on other fish, notably herring.

Breeding Similar to the Pollack. The immature fish are known as billet. Like Pollack young, they remain inshore and are locally common.

Distribution More northerly distribution than the Pollack, favouring deeper water on both sides of the Atlantic.

POOR COD

Trisopterus minutus

A small member of the cod family that favours rocky bottoms but will range over sand and muddy seabeds in its search for food.

Appearance Length rarely exceeds 25 cm. Distinct resemblance to the Pouting (see p. 130): reddish colouring but no vertical bars of darker shading and no dark blotch at the root of the pectoral fins.

Feeding Microscopic organisms and minor invertebrates.

Breeding Spawns during the spring. Little else is known.

Distribution Throughout the North Atlantic.

TORSK

Brosme brosme

A fish of northern waters, the Torsk frequents deep waters off the Scottish coast.

Appearance Length 110 cm; weight 5kg. Dull bronze back, fading to a creamy belly. A single dorsal fin which, along with the anal fin, is fused with the fish's tail. Elongated barbule beneath the chin.

Feeding Demersal in habit, feeding mainly on crustaceans.

Breeding Spawns in very deep water (at 500 m) during late spring, where a huge number of eggs are shed. Eggs are pelagic and hatch in about two weeks.

Distribution Scotland, Iceland, Norway and the Arctic region.

BLUE WHITING *Micromesistius poutassou*

A fish of the open ocean, the Blue Whiting inhabits deep water. The species is a future source of human food but, as yet, little harvesting of the fish takes place. At present, the fish are used to process into fishmeal.

Appearance Length 50 cm. Resembles the common Whiting (see p. 131) but slimmer, the three dorsal fins spaced further apart. Underjaw noticeably longer; eyes large.

Feeding Crustaceans and tiny fish.

Breeding See Whiting (p.131).

Distribution From Norway, down through the Mediterranean to Asia Minor.

LING

Molva molva

The Ling inhabits deep water and the rough seabed, favouring reefs, wrecks and areas that provide good ambush opportunities. When mature, the species lives an almost solitary existence, not forming shoals.

Appearance Length 220 cm; weight 20 kg. Probably the largest-growing of the cod family. Dark brown-black on the upper parts, with silvery flanks. Mature fish have a mottling of dark blotches on the sides. One anal and two dorsal fins, with a clear white banding around the frilled, outer edges. Large barbule under the chin; mouth is full of sharp teeth, indicating a predator on other fish.

Feeding Other species of fish, e.g. whiting, pouting, gurnards, crustaceans.

Breeding Prolific spawner, laying up to 60 million eggs in late spring.

Distribution Throughout the eastern Atlantic.

HAKE

Merluccius merluccius

The Hake has been subjected to massive overfishing, so few are caught today. The situation may be improving, but more rigid control of species quotas within the European Union is vital.

Appearance Length 140 cm; weight 12 kg. Like the Ling (see p. 137), has only two dorsal fins and an elongated anal fin, but is less eel-like with no barbule. Mouth is large with extremely sharp teeth. Scales are large and distinct and easily removed by abrasion.

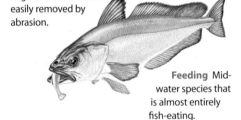

Feeding Mid-water species that is almost entirely fish-eating.

Breeding Spawns out in the Atlantic Ocean in a depth of about 200 m. The eggs are pelagic, wholly dependent on warm currents to drift them in towards the shallow, fertile feeding areas.

Distribution In the N Atlantic as far south as Portugal.

GREATER FORKBEARD

Phycis blennoides

The Greater Forkbeard lives in deep water and forms large shoals. Breeding habits are unknown.

Appearance Length 110 cm. Dull brown on the upper body shading to a white belly. Two dorsal and one anal fin. Pelvic fins reduced to thin, trailing appendages that flow rearwards to touch the anal fin. Large eyes and a long barbule on the chin.

Feeding Feeds on small crustaceans and bottom-living fish.

Distribution Thinly distributed in the open Atlantic but very common in the Mediterranean.

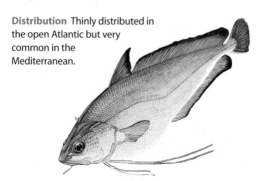

ROCKLINGS

The rocklings are a group of secretive fishes related to the cod family. The behaviour and chosen environments vary enormously between the different species. There are five rockling species distributed around the British coast:

Three-bearded Rockling *Gaidropsarus vulgarus*
Four-bearded Rockling *Rhinonemus cimbrius*
Five-bearded Rockling *Ciliata mustela*
Northern Rockling *Ciliata septentrionalis*
Shore Rockling *Gaidropsarus mediterraneus*

Appearance Length 25–60 cm. Very few anatomical differences between species; resemble immature Ling (see p. 137) and are often mistaken for the young of that larger, deepwater fish, except that they have barbules on the upper jaw. Large mouths with sharp teeth. Each species has two dorsal and one anal fin. First dorsal fin is rudimentary and lies folded in a cleft on the fish's back. Number and position of barbules on the upper jaw varies between species; only the single chin barbule is common to all.

Feeding Nocturnal feeders, eating all slow-moving creatures, fish, worms and other invertebrates.

Breeding During spring and summer. Little else is known.

Distribution Around the British Isles and north-eastern Atlantic.

4-bearded Rockling

5-bearded Rockling

3-bearded Rockling

Northern Rockling

TADPOLE FISH   *Raniceps raninus*

Also called the Lesser Forkbeard, this rare minor cod
inhabits shallow waters where it lives a solitary
existence among rocks and kelp. Its breeding habits
are unknown.

Appearance Length 30 cm. Resembling a tadpole,
body is dark brown with a large and flattened head.
First dorsal fin is composed of only a few short rays.
Second dorsal fin and the anal fin both extremely
long. Small barbule and thin, elongated pelvic fins.

Feeding Worms and small crustaceans.

Distribution Coasts of British Isles and France
north to Norway.

SUNFISH *Mola mola*

Though a weak swimmer, the Sunfish has a worldwide distribution. The species is carried along on the ocean currents, making sluggish paddling movements with its fins.

Appearance Length 300 cm. A peculiar fish with one dorsal and anal fin, a tiny mouth and no evidence of a tail. Deep-bodied and flattened laterally with the rear part of the body ending in a muscular frilling. Bronze/dark brown colouring with lighter underparts.

Feeding Feeds pelagically on slow-moving larvae in the plankton layers.

Breeding Thought to spawn in and around the Sargasso Sea, where each female deposits over 100,000 eggs.

Distribution Worldwide, though not in arctic waters.

OPAH
Lampris guttatus

Often called the Ocean Moonfish, this species is distributed worldwide. Opah are pelagic fish that drift northward during the summer months on the warm current stream. They are rarely seen but are caught, accidentally, in surface nets. Breeding habits and precise distribution are unknown.

Appearance Length 180 cm. Beautifully coloured: purple-blue ground and vermillion-red fins, body deep and laterally compressed. Small mouth with thick, rubbery lips capable of tubelike extension.

Feeding Mainly squid found among plankton.

JOHN DORY

Zeus faber

A striking fish of unique shape and colouring, the John Dory favours warm, shallow waters.

Appearance Length 66 cm; weight 2.5 kg. Bronze back and flanks, lighter blue and yellowish marbling on the flanks. Deep body, laterally compressed. Mouth is huge and shoots forward into a kind of suction tube. Two dorsal fins, the first supported by stiff spines. Single spine in the pelvic fins and four in the first section of the anal fin. Dark blotch on the flanks makes identification certain.

Feeding Fish – for example sardines, sprats and other small pelagic species.

Breeding Spawns in warm waters of high summer. Little else is known.

Distribution Warm regions of eastern Atlantic.

BOARFISH

Capros aper

Similar in shape to the John Dory (see p. 145), the Boarfish gets its name from its pig-like snout! Its feeding and breeding habits are unknown.

Appearance Length 18 cm. Less vivid in colouring than the John Dory but fins are also spined.

Distribution Found in warm areas south and west of the British Isles.

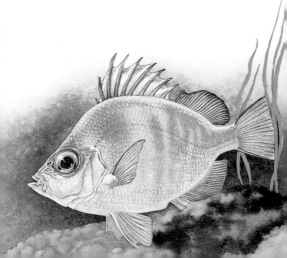

HORSE MACKEREL   *Trachurus trachurus*

This widespread visitor, also known as the Scad, is no relation to the true Mackerel (see p. 148-9) but can often be found accompanying mackerel shoals inshore. It is a member of the family Carangidae and is of economic importance in southern Africa.

Appearance Length 60 cm; weight 1.9 kg. Can be identified by the row of bony plates along its flanks. Greenish-grey body, with a spined first dorsal fin and two sharp spines ahead of the anal fin. Tail is deeply forked and the pectoral fins curved, ending in a sharp point. Dark blotch high on the gill case.

Feeding Pelagic-living fry of other species of fish.

Breeding Spawns in summer in British waters but later (winter) in the open ocean. Fry are frequently found sheltering among the tentacles of the jellyfish *Rhizostoma*, and feed on jellyfish parasites.

Distribution The whole Atlantic seaboard from Norway to South Africa.

MACKEREL

Scomber scombrus

One of the fastest swimmers in the sea, the Mackerel is a member of the tunny family. The species can be regarded as pelagic-feeding, ocean wanderers for much of each year. In early summer huge shoals move into the shallow, coastal waters to harry the fry of other species. Then, as autumn and winter arrive, the fish leave for deeper water offshore, where, it is stated, they rest and do not feed. Here they find no security, however, for massive predation by deep-water trawling in winter by a number of European countries has decimated the once-prolific shoals. The Mackerel is one of our best-known table fish and the demand for ever-increasing catches is formidable.

Appearance Length 50 cm; weight 1.8 kg. Back has a brilliant metallic greeny-blue sheen. This ground colour is patterned, dorsally, by a mass of black twisting lines. Blotches of colour on the lighter, pale green flanks; white underparts have scales that flash in the light with a myriad hues. Built for speed, body is streamlined with small fins, some of which fold into grooves, so presenting less surface drag as the fish speeds through the water. Mouth can be tightly closed against the ingress of water and eyes are set in sockets, flush to the head, so as not to protrude outside the tapering body shape. Tail is deeply forked with a pair of keels at the roof. Tiny finlets on the back and belly after the second dorsal and anal fin. Sharp spine behind the vent which, though hard to detect, can easily cut into a person's hand. Mackerel have no swim bladders.

Feeding Fry of other species of fish together with zooplankton.

Breeding Spawning begins in May in the upper, warmer water layers and eggs hatch in about a week.

Distribution Throughout the Atlantic Ocean.

RED MULLET   *Mullus surmuletus*

The Red Mullet is a species with a misleading common name; the fish in fact belongs to the tropical goatfish family. It inhabits shallow waters.

Appearance Length 40 cm.
Brilliant colouring; its large scales of red/orange fading to yellow make it unique. Flattened forehead and long trailing barbules, which are used to detect food.

Feeding Small invertebrates and other organisms found in mud and sand.

Breeding On occasion the red mullet breeds in British Isles waters, though its normal habitat is more southerly, warmer seas.

Distribution The entire Mediterranean Sea and European coast, north to southern England and Ireland.

RAY'S BREAM   *Brama brama*

This fish is known worldwide but can be termed only a sporadic visitor to the British Isles. Single specimens are washed ashore, mostly in winter, perhaps due to exceptional warmth in north-flowing currents earlier in the year. This was noted by the naturalist, John Ray, who gave the fish its common name in the 17th century. Its feeding and breeding habits are unknown.

Appearance Length 70 cm; weight 2.5 kg. Deep body, laterally compressed, indicating a life spent at considerable depths. Deep brown in colour, the flanks have a metallic, flashing quality to the scaling. Very sharp teeth.

Distribution Uncommon in Britain; very common off the coasts of Spain and Portugal.

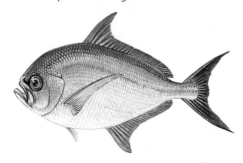

BASS

Dincentrachus labrax

This is one of the best-known sporting fish. Renowned for feeding in the breaking surf of the open storm beaches, the Bass is found on most European southern and west-facing shores. The more northerly areas attract solitary but large specimens, whereas warmer sea areas are populated by smaller, 'school' Bass. The Bass has a tolerance for brackish water and will often be found in the estuaries of large rivers, where it can be confused with similar-looking grey mullet. Bass are slow to mature and over-fishing is endangering the species. Efforts to curb the commercial fishing pressures have yet to produce any worthwhile results. However, there is some evidence, in Ireland, that Bass are slowly returning.

Appearance Length 100 cm; weight 7.5 kg. Powerful, thickset, muscular body; dark green-black on the back with silvery flanks and a creamy belly. Scales are hard and rough to the touch, with a spiny, ctenoid hind margin. First dorsal fin is spined; second has soft, jointed rays. Three spines at the leading edge of the anal fin and a single spine on each of the paired, pelvic fins. Edge of the gill case has a sharp plate.

Feeding Searches mudflats for invertebrates and crustaceans.

Breeding Little is known about spawning time or behaviour. It may be that Bass spawn over a protracted period, shedding a number of eggs when and where conditions appear favourable. Still less is known about the annual migration to deep water; some winter catches made off the Eddystone Rock suggest that this predator seeks the larger food supplies of offshore reefs during the cold months. On the Atlantic shores of Ireland, Bass are present throughout the winter, the warmer oceanic water offering a more stable environment.

Distribution It is a warm water species in the British Isles, tending to be found in shoals on western Atlantic shores as far north as the Solway Firth. Widespread on the south coast and moves up into the North Sea to the Yorkshire coast and Friesian Islands off Holland.

BLACK SEA BREAM
Spondyliosoma cantharus

A summer visitor to North Atlantic waters, the Black Sea Bream is most often recorded from the English Channel, off the Sussex and Hampshire coasts. There are more than 200 species occurring in warm summer seas, within the sea bream family.

Appearance Length 60 cm. Deep, compressed body, purple-grey in colour with streaks of horizontal bands of golden scales below the lateral line. No dark spot above the pectoral fins (see Red Sea Bream, p. 155). Dorsal fin is long with 11 spined rays and 12–14 soft, branched rays.

Feeding Crustaceans and invertebrates, small fish fry.

Breeding Breeds in the winter months far to the south. Little else is known.

Distribution All sea breams are widely distributed in the Mediterranean.

RED SEA BREAM   *Pagellus bogaraveo*

The Red Sea Bream travels in shoals and frequents rocky ground. See Black Sea Bream (p.154) for Feeding and Breeding.

Appearance Length 70 cm; weight 3.5 kg. Less deep than the Black Sea Bream in its body, identification points are the red fins, golden-red scales, large eyes and dark shoulder patch.

Distribution Similar distribution to the Black Sea Bream (see p.154), though it can be found in more northerly areas.

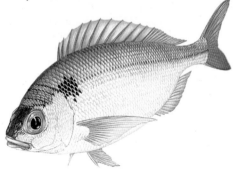

BALLAN WRASSE   *Labrus bergylta*

Found in shallow water around rocky coastline. During the winter Ballan Wrasse escape the cold by retiring to deeper water offshore with a rocky ground habitat.

Appearance Length 60 cm; weight 4.3 kg. Coloration varies greatly but green, brown and red predominate. Often an orange patch under throat; some fish exhibit a lattice-work pattern of red-brown lines across shoulders and head. Solid, thickset body with large fins, prominent lips and clearly defined ark-edged scales. Teeth are chisel-shaped, used to tear molluscs from rocks.

Feeding Molluscs and crustaceans found among the boulders and kelpbeds of the littoral zone.

Breeding Breeds in early summer, building nests of tufted seaweeds in rock crevices.

Distribution Coastline of European Atlantic.

CUCKOO WRASSE
Labrus mixtus

This is a slimmer, more colourful member of the wrasse family with a longer snout. Less common than the Ballan Wrasse (see p. 156), the Cuckoo Wrasse is found in similar habitats but in much deeper water. Often this smaller wrasse will be caught in lobster and crab pots, from which it steals the bait. See Ballan Wrasse for Feeding and Breeding.

Appearance Length 35 cm; weight 1 kg. Like the Ballan Wrasse, the gill case is scaled and the jaw teeth strong and pointed. Powerful, grinding molars at the throat entrance. Cuckoo Wrasse display a sexual colour difference which used to cause problems of identification: males are brilliant blue on head and upper body; belly and fins bright orange hue. Streaks and marbled pattern of darker blue extend back from the head and gill case. Females are reddish-orange with dark blotches beneath the rear section of the dorsal fin.

female

Distribution Atlantic seaboard.

male

GOLDSINNY *Ctenolabrus rupestris*

A very small member of the wrasse family that lives in shallow, coastal waters. The species is widely distributed in areas with a rocky seabed. See Ballan Wrasse (p. 156) for colouring and Feeding. Little is known about its breeding habits.

Appearance Length 18 cm. Can be identified by the dark blotch at the beginning of the dorsal fin and a similar spot at the top of the fore-edge of the tail fin.

Distribution Coastal waters throughout Europe.

RAINBOW WRASSE
Coris julis

This colourful wrasse is rarely found north of the English Channel, although it is common in warm coastal waters further south. See Ballan Wrasse (p. 156) for Feeding and Breeding.

Appearance Length 25 cm. Alone among the wrasse, Rainbow Wrasse has sharply pointed fins and lacks scaling on the gill case and cheeks. Colouring variable: males have purple-green upper parts, shading to silvery-yellow flanks; females display a muted variation with narrow, lighter, lateral stripes.

Distribution Coastal areas of Europe; common in the Mediterranean.

ROCK COOK   *Centrolabrus exoletus*

A small wrasse found in more northern climes, around the British Isles and along the coast of Norway. Little is known about its feeding and breeding habits or about precise distribution. Very small examples have been taken in rock pools and lobster fishermen have found them within their pots, possibly feeding on scraps of lobster bait.

Appearance Length 15 cm. A duller version of the Ballan Wrasse (see p. 156) in colouring. Small mouth; five spined rays in the fore-edge of the anal fin.

CORKWING WRASSE *Crenilabrus melops*

Found from Norway to the Black Sea, this small wrasse has vast variation it its coloration. Little is known about its feeding and breeding habits.

Appearance Length 28 cm. Small fish resembling the Ballan Wrasse (see p. 156) but more thickset, often with two dark blotches of colour; one at the root of the tail and the other at the rear of the eye.

Distribution Coastal waters of Norway, down to Spain.

GREATER WEEVER   *Trachinus draco*

The Greater Weever frequents deeper water offshore than the Lesser Weever (see p. 163). Little is known about its breeding habits. Like all weevers, it is venomous. Weevers can inflict a painful wound with their spined dorsal fins, which have poison sacs located at the base. The first dorsal spine is the dangerous one and care must be taken to avoid the spines on the gill case of the Greater Weever. Medical advice should always be sought if you are stung by a weever or similar-looking fish.

Appearance Length 40 cm. Two or three times the size of the Lesser Weever. Slimmer body with spots and streaks over a grey-blue ground colour.

Feeding Small fish of many demersal species.

Breeding Little is known about breeding habits.

Distribution Norway, down the African coast and the length of the Mediterranean.

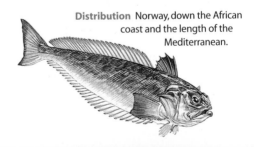

LESSER WEEVER   *Trachinus vipera*

The Lesser Weever is a tiny fish found in shallow water, in places where there are gently sloping sandy beaches. Like the Greater Weever (see p.162), it is venomous and medical advice should always be sought if you are stung.

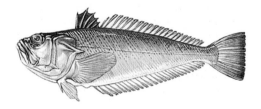

Appearance Length 18–20 cm. It lies partly buried in the sand, with the dorsal spines erected. Weevers feed on minute invertebrates and fish larvae.

Feeding Small fish of many demersal species.

Breeding Little is known about breeding habits.

Distribution Norway, down the African coast and the length of the Mediterranean.

WOLF-FISH

Anarhichas lupus

This large, ugly, bottom-dwelling fish is often called a Catfish or Sea-cat. Its chosen environment is deep water over a rocky seabed. Wolf-fish are highly prized among commercial fisherman as the flesh is tasty and the fish can grow to a considerable size: fish of 2.4 m and more have been landed. They form a large part of the catch in northern waters. In the fish market they are sold as 'Rock Salmon', a title that is also shared by the ubiquitous Coalfish (see p. 131).

Appearance Length 125 cm; weight 5 kg. Body is drab green-grey, with faint brown marbling on the flanks and fins. Long, grilled dorsal fin extending from behind the head, back to the tail. Anal fin begins at the vent and ends just below the posterior edge of the dorsal. Pectoral fins are huge rounded paddles. No pelvic fins and scales are rudimentary. Head is blunt and the large mouth has curved canine teeth on the upper and lower jaws. Behind the lower canines are a series of smaller molars. Also teeth in the roof of the mouth. This fearsome armoury is needed to cope with the demersal crustaceans it feeds on.

Feeding Chiefly crabs, lobsters and shellfish.

Breeding Spawns during winter; eggs are laid in

groups on the seabed where they hatch after two months.

Distribution Found on both sides of the North Atlantic in temperate and arctic seas.

BLUEFIN TUNNY   *Thunnus thynnus*

The Bluefin Tunny prefers warmer climes, although after spawning this species does migrate into northern seas to feed. A food fish of worldwide importance, it is rarely seen inshore. It is also among the finest of big-game sporting fishes.

Appearance Length 300 cm; weight 435 kg. Deep-bodied and powerful. Dark blue body, almost black on the back, shading to silvery-white on the belly.

Feeding Pelagic oceanic hunter that travels widely, preying on shoals of baitfish.

Breeding Tunny spawn in the Mediterranean Sea during June, after which they travel far, often to Norwegian waters, in search of shoals of large fish upon which they feed and recover from the rigours of breeding.

Distribution The warm and tropical waters of the world.

BROADBILL SWORDFISH
Xiphias gladius

This species is allied to the Mackerel and the Bluefin Tunny (see pp. 148 and 166). Many tales are told of Swordfish that have attacked wooden ships, but the occurrences were probably accidental.

Appearance Length 450 cm; weight 150 kg. Dull blue shading almost to light grey on the belly. Elongated upper jaw is formed into a flattened bill. Two widely spaced dorsal fins and a small keel on either side of the tail wrist.

Feeding Squid and fish of many species.

Breeding Spawns in equatorial water in summer. Though a large fish, eggs are very small, just over 1.5 mm. Hatching Swordfish are voracious hunters in the pelagic zone.

Distribution Tropical and temperate zones.

BLUEMOUTH *Heliconelus dactylopterus*

This fish is more southerly in distribution than the Norway Haddock (see p.169) and is found in deep water.

Appearance Length 45 cm. Very similar to Norway Haddock, can be identified by the blue tint inside the mouth, and the very large pectoral fins.

Feeding Feeds on bottom-dwelling crustaceans, worms and other invertebrates.

Breeding Viviparous, producing several thousand larval offspring each summer.

Distribution Around the Scottish coast and off the west of Ireland.

NORWAY HADDOCK

Sebastes viviparus

The Norway Haddock is found in deep water (down to 300 m) over a rough seabed.

Appearance Length 35 cm. Stumpy, thickset body, brilliant red in coloration. Spiny gill case and first portion to dorsal fin. Huge eyes dominate the large head.

Feeding Bottom-feeding species seeking crustaceans and invertebrates.

Breeding See Bluemouth (p. 168).

Distribution An occasional visitor to northern Scotland, found in waters off Iceland, Norway and occasionally western Ireland.

RED GURNARD
Aspitrigla cuculu

This species is found in a wide variety of habitats within European Atlantic waters.

Appearance Length 50 cm; weight 1.4 kg. All gurnards possess armoured bones covering the heads. Pectoral fins are divided into two distinct sections. The three leading rays are separate, stiffened tactile organs also used to aid walking around on the seabed. First dorsal fin is tall and spined and gurnard tails are deeply forked. Red Gurnard has a series of vertical plates along the lateral line. Like other gurnards, it can make a noise – a croaking sound (see Grey Gurnard, p. 172).

Feeding Feeds on demersal fish, crustaceans and various invertebrates.

Breeding Eggs are layed from late April to the end of summer. Hatching occurs within two weeks and the young feed on zooplankton.

Distibution From the Black Sea to the British Isles.

TUB GURNARD

Trigla lucerna

A larger-growing gurnard but scarcer than its red cousin, this species comes into shallow waters more readily. See Red Gurnard (p. 170) for Feeding, Breeding and Distribution.

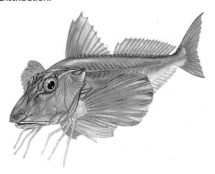

Appearance See also Red Gurnard. Length 75 cm; weight 5 kg. Coloration is variable, which causes identification problems, but the huge pectoral fins, stretching rearwards beyond the vent, are distinctive: bright orange with an edging of brilliant blue. There may also be a number of dark blotches on these fins. Almost smooth lateral line, with only a slight ridging effect.

GREY GURNARD   *Eutrigla gurnardus*

The most common of the gurnard family, this small fish is found as far north as the Arctic Circle. Inhabiting shallow water during summer months, the fish, like all other gurnards, is said to 'croak' when taken from the water. This noise is produced by the swim bladder and is used, presumably, to signal to other fish. See Red Gurnard (p. 170) for Feeding and Breeding.

Appearance See also Red Gurnard. Length 50 cm; weight 1 kg. Colouring is variable from grey to a dull red, usually with lighter spots on back and flanks. Prickly lateral line and a series of prickles at either side of the groove into which dorsal fins are set.

Distribution Murmansk to the Black Sea, around the Atlantic coast.

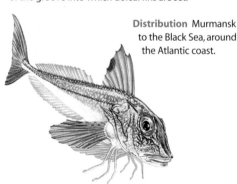

LANTERN GURNARD *Aspitrigla obscura*

This is a rare, deep-water species of gurnard. Little is known about its feeding and breeding habits. Distribution is probably similar to that of other gurnards.

Appearance See also Red Gurnard (p.170). Length 40 cm. Distinguished by first dorsal fin, which has a much higher second spine than any of the other gurnards.

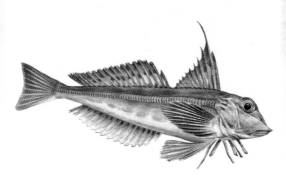

PIPER GURNARD
Trigla lyra

Like the Lantern Gurnard (see p. 173), this fish favours deep water. See Red Gurnard (p. 170) for Feeding and Breeding.

Appearance See also Red Gurnard. Length 60 cm. Long spines protrude back from the gill cases above the pectoral fins, and connected spines that form forward projections from the upper jaw.

Distribution Found in more southerly waters than the Red or Tub Gurnard (see p. 171).

STREAKED GURNARD
Trigloporus lastoviza

This is a widely distributed fish in European waters.

Appearance See also Red Gurnard (p.170). Length 40 cm. Blunt head, streaks of colour and vertical lines on the body identify the Streaked Gurnard.

Feeding Feeds on demersal fish, crustaceans and various invertebrates.

Breeding Eggs are layed from late April to the end of summer. Hatching occurs within two weeks and the young feed on zooplankton.

Distibution From the Black Sea to the British Isles.

SHORT-SPINED SEA SCORPION
Myoxocephalus scorpius

The Short-spined Sea Scorpion or Father Lasher inhabits littoral waters, swimming almost to the tideline.

Appearance Length 40 cm. Small, colourful fish with numerous spines on the body, gill case and first dorsal fin.

Feeding Invertebrates and fish larvae.

Breeding Spawns in April–July, laying eggs in clumps, which the male fish guards until they hatch.

Distribution Widespread across the Atlantic and up into arctic waters.

LONG-SPINED SEA SCORPION
Taurulus bubalis

Appearance Length 17.5 cm. Small, colourful fish with numerous spines on the body, gill case and first dorsal fin.

Feeding Invertebrates and fish larvae.

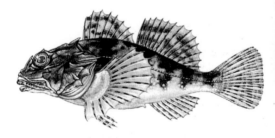

Breeding Spawns in April–July, laying eggs in clumps, which the male fish guards until they hatch.

Distribution From the Bay of Biscay to northern Norway.

DRAGONET

Callionymus lyra

This is a common, slender fish of shallow sandy areas.

Appearance Length 30 cm (male), 25 cm (female). Male highly colourful with an elongated, spined first dorsal fin; female drab brown with smaller fins.

Feeding Small shellfish and crustaceans.

Breeding Spawns early in the year, when the male fish performs a ritual dance to encourage egg laying!

Distribution Western Europe coastline.

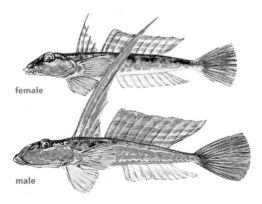

female

male

FIFTEEN-SPINED STICKLEBACK
Spinachia spinachia

The sticklebacks are unique in that there are two species that favour living in freshwater (see pp. 72–3). This third stickleback, also called the Sea Stickleback, however, spends its entire lifecycle in the north European coastal waters.

Appearance Length 19 cm. Very different from freshwater species in body shape; 14–17 spines precede the dorsal fin, positioned halfway along the slender body. Colour varies according to the chosen rocky habitat but olive-yellow predominates.

Feeding Very small invertebrates and, possibly, the eggs of other fish.

Breeding Spawns early summer; builds nest among clumps of seaweed, tying the fronds together with mucus. Unlike other sticklebacks, forms a pair bond, the female laying her eggs in a nest guarded by the male.

Distribution European littoral waters.

VIVIPAROUS BLENNY *Zoarces viviparus*

Also known as the Eelpout, this is a very common fish of European littoral waters that can be found hiding among seaweeds and stones in the algal zone.

Appearance Length 52 cm; weight 1.25 kg. Colour varies with environment but generally an olive-brown base with darker marbling. Dorsal fin is continuous between head and tail, posterior section low and with a number of weak spined rays.

Feeding Young feed on minute invertebrates and inshore plankton, adult fish add worms and molluscs to the diet.

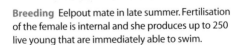

Breeding Eelpout mate in late summer. Fertilisation of the female is internal and she produces up to 250 live young that are immediately able to swim.

Distribution British Isles north to Norway, south to Brest peninsula.

YARRELL'S BLENNY *Chirolophis ascanii*

Like the Viviparous Blenny (see p. 180), this is another small fish of rocky, inshore waters where it lives among the seaweeds.

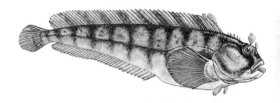

Appearance Length 25 cm. Body long and slender with two tentacles on the head, above the eyes. More tentacles on the tips of the first dorsal fin spines. Colour is reddish-brown with dark mottling along the flanks.

Feeding Marine worms and small invertebrates.

Breeding This species is egg-laying, which takes place in early winter.

Distribution Around the British Isles, Norway and northern France.

MONTAGU'S BLENNY
Coryphoblennius galerita

This is a minor species of blenny.

Appearance Length rarely more than 7 cm. Small and thickset, with tentacles above the eyes.

Feeding Minute invertebrates.

Breeding Female deposits eggs in crevices and rock pools.

Distribution Around the British Isles, Norway and northern France.

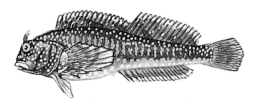

TOMPOT BLENNY *Blennius gattorugine*

Like Montagu's Blenny (see p. 182), this is another minor species, although growing to at least twice the length of *galerita*.

Appearance Length 30 cm. Thickset, with tentacles above the eyes.

Feeding Minute invertebrates.

Breeding Female deposits eggs in crevices and rock pools.

Distribution Around the British Isles, Norway and northern France.

PAINTED GOBY   *Pomatoschistus pictus*

The gobies are a large family of small, coastal-dwelling fish that thrive in shallow waters. They are able to cope with powerful wave action as they have pelvic fins fused together to form a suction pad which allows the tiny fish to stick themselves to rocks or other supports.

Appearance Length up to 6 cm. Two rows of highly coloured spots on the dorsal fins and brown blotches along the body.

Feeding Minute invertebrates.

Breeding Spawning takes place in the height of summer. Eggs are laid on weeds or in open shells, where they are guarded by the male fish.

Distribution On rocky coasts throughout the North Atlantic.

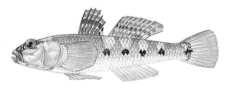

SAND GOBY   *Pomatoschistus minutus*

The Sand Goby grows to about the same size as other small gobies. See Painted Goby (p. 184) for a general description and for Feeding, Breeding and Distribution.

Appearance Length 6.5 cm. Black patch on the posterior edge of the first dorsal.

BLACK GOBY   *Gobius niger*

See Painted Goby (p. 184) for a general description and for Feeding, Breeding and Distribution.

Appearance Length 15 cm. Brown rather than black in colour with close-set dorsal fins.

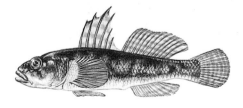

GREATER SANDEEL
Hyperoplus lanceolatus

Sandeels are shoalfish that live over offshore sandbanks. Widely distributed, they are preyed upon by most of the important food fish and form a major part of of the oceanic life support system.

Appearance Length 40 cm. Slender, eel-like in shape, with one long dorsal fin and a forked tail. Green back, flanks shading to silver. Dark patch at either side of the elongated snout.

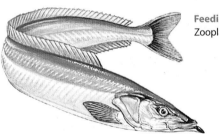

Feeding Zooplankton.

Breeding Breeds in the summer, eggs hatching in about 18 days.

Distribution Widespread from the Bay of Biscay to the Arctic North Cape.

LESSER SANDEEL   *Ammodytes tobianus*

Found in similar habitats to the Greater Sandeel (see p. 186), this common species will bury itself in gently sloping sandy beaches as the tide recedes. It is often dug up to be used as food or fisherman's bait.

Appearance Length 20 cm. Slender, eel-like in shape, with one long dorsal fin and a forked tail. Green back, flanks shading to silver. Dark patch at either side of the elongated snout.

Feeding Zooplankton.

Breeding Spawns from late summer, into autumn.

Distribution Widespread from the Bay of Biscay to the Arctic North Cape.

LUMPSUCKER
Cyclopterus lumpus

The Lumpsucker is an awkward fish, aptly named. It favours rocky ground in shallow areas. It is said that its eggs can be used to produce a kind of second-rate caviar.

Appearance Length 51 cm (male), 61 cm (female); weight 5 kg. Sexual/colour variation: males are blue-black on back and sides with a reddish tinge on the underbelly; females are muted grey-blue. In both sexes dorsal fin is set far back behind a ridge of bony tubercles. Body is liberally covered in tubercles, the largest being formed into three lateral rows along the flanks. Pelvic fins are fused to form a suction disc which enables the fish to adhere to rocks on the seabed.

Feeding Invertebrates, crustaceans and the fry of demersal fishes.

Breeding Spawns in the spring, after establishing a pair bond, and lays a huge number of eggs. Male fish guard the eggs until they hatch

Distribution Found throughout the North Atlantic.

GUNNEL

Pholis gunnellus

This small-growing species, also known as the Butterfish, lives in shallow waters that offer weed and rocky areas of security. Beloved by children exploring the beach and rockpools, the Butterfish is difficult to pick up – hence its name.

Appearance Length 25 cm. Easily recognised by eel-like shape; body generally grey with a dorsal fin from head to tail. Its anal fin is half its body length. Series of black spots, edged with white, at base of dorsal fin.

Feeding Minute organisms and tiny crustaceans.

Breeding Breeds during the winter, eggs laid in crevices or among stones where both parents guard them.

Distribution Throughout the North Atlantic

POGGE
Agonus cataphractus

Sometimes call the Armed Bullhead, this fish appears to be a relic from prehistoric times. The species is demersal and lives among weedgrowth on soft seabeds.

Appearance Length 21 cm. Body seems to be divided by ridges of armoured plates. Group of stiff bristles under the chin and around the mouth. First dorsal fin is spined and the supporting rays of all fins are speckled with dark brown colouring.

Feeding Small crustaceans and molluscs.

Breeding Breeds in early spring. The eggs have a very lengthy hatching time – almost a year!

Distribution British Isles and North Sea up to Norway.

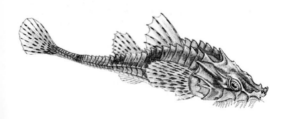

WRECKFISH   *Polyprion americanus*

This is a large fish, solitary in behaviour, haunting rocky ground in deep water. Its breeding habits are unknown.

Appearance Length 200 cm; weight 100 kg. Colour varies between brown-red and dirty yellow. One long dorsal fin: forward portion has stiff spines, joined with leathery webs, followed by soft rays. Anal fin is short and set far back on the body. Prominent bony ridge on each gill case. Extremely small scales for a fish of its size.

Feeding Predates on pelagic fry found hiding among floating weeds and flotsam.

Distribution
Throughout tropical and temperate areas of the Atlantic.

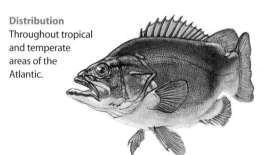

THIN-LIPPED MULLET   *Liza ramada*

Mullet are summer visitors. All three species (see pp. 192-4) can be found haunting harbours, where they glide, almost unseen, through the shadows of the boats, scavenging for titbits among the flotsam. In shallow estuarine areas, the fish swim with their dorsal fins cutting the surface film. Mullet are important food for Europe, particularly countries around the Mediterranean.

Appearance See also Thick-Lipped Mullet (p.193). Length 60 cm. Large silver scales, darkening to almost black on the fish's back. No lateral line in evidence. Narrow upper lip and a broad throat slit. Elongated pectoral fins.

Feeding Plankton, small invertebrates and weeds.

Breeding Spawns in spring but little else is known.

Distribution Move north from the Mediterranean and Iberian Peninsula to British coastal waters and the shores of France, Belgium and Holland in late spring.

THICK-LIPPED MULLET
Crenimugil labrosus

Appearance Length 90 cm; weight 3.5 kg. Thickened upper lip and a very narrow throat slit. Both this species and the Thin-lipped Mullet have a distinctive first dorsal fin with four spined rays. There is no lateral line.

Feeding Plankton, small invertebrates and weeds.

Breeding Spawns in spring but little else is known.

Distribution Move north from the Mediterranean and Iberian Peninsula to British coastal waters and the shores of France, Belgium and Holland in late spring.

GOLDEN-GREY MULLET *Liza auratus*

This fish is less northerly in distribution than the other two mullet species (see pp. 192-3), rarely found north of the British Isles. See these entries for Feeding and Breeding.

Appearance Length 50 cm. Beautiful golden sheen to the scales on its flanks and underbelly. Cheek patch of bright yellow. Upper lip is thin and the species exhibits a broad throat slit. Elongated pectoral fins. In shape, it resembles the other two species.

Distribution Throughout the Mediterranean Sea and up to the British Isles.

SHANNY
Blennius pholis

An ugly little fish of the rocky coastline, it is often found in rock pools, where it jealously guards its territory from other small invaders.

Appearance Length 16 cm. Grey-green coloration is blotched with brown, black and cream. Anal fin has light edging. Behind the broad head, dorsal extends to the tail with a pronounced cut-out section in the middle.

Feeding Small invertebrates and molluscs

Breeding Breeds among rocks and weedbeds of the littoral zone.

Distribution All rocky coastal areas in western Europe.

FLATFISH:
Left- and Right-Handedness

All flatfish are either left or right-handed. Both eyes are to the right of the mouth in a left-handed fish and to the left of the mouth in a right-handed fish. There are a few exceptions, such as the Flounder (see p. 208), which is generally right-handed, although left-handed Flounders are very common – but these fish cannot be regarded as normal.

After hatching from the egg in the upper layers of the sea, all flatfish are symmetrical with an eye on each side of the tiny body. As they grow, feeding on plankton, the body deepens, some blotches of colour appear and one eye migrates around the head to join the other on the coloured side. At this stage in the metamorphosis the flatfish larvae will have descended to begin a benthic, bottom-dwelling existence. The 'blind side' remains colourless in all but a few individuals that may display albinism (white 'coloured' sides) or ambi-coloration (where part of the blind side bears pigmentation).

LEFT-HANDED FISH

Bothidae:
Scaldfish

Scophthalmidae:
Turbot, Brill, Megrim
and Topknot

RIGHT-HANDED FISH

Pleuronectidae:
Halibut, Greenland
Halibut, Dab, Long
Rough Dab, Plaice,
Flounder, Lemon Sole
and Witch

Solidae: Sole (or Dover
Sole) and Solenette
(right-handed species
but not related to other
flatfish)

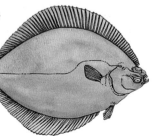

TURBOT   *Scophthalmus maximus*

The largest of the left-handed flatfish, the Turbot lives over sandbanks and other mixed ground.

Appearance Length 90 cm; weight 15 kg. Thick, fleshy, round-shaped body with a broad, powerful tail fin. Upper, coloured side has a number of bony tubercles extending out to the body margins. Underneath it lacks scales and is nearly pure white in colour. Dorsal fin begins just in front of the upper eye and the lateral line takes a pronounced curve over the pectoral fin. Mouth is capable of lengthy protrusion, a necessary aid to feeding as it is not a fast fish.

Feeding Feeds largely on live fish, which it catches as they are swept along in currents.

Breeding See also Flatfish (p. 166-7). Spawns in late-spring and summer, producing millions of eggs.

Distribution Western Atlantic and into the Mediterranean and Baltic Seas.

BRILL
Scophthalmus rhombus

A close relative to the Turbot (see p. 198), it frequents similar habitats.

Appearance Length 75 cm; weight 3.5 kg. Smaller-growing, thinner through the body than the Turbot, with no tubercles. Skin is covered with minute scales over a mottled grey-brown base coloration.

Feeding Small fish and crustaceans.

Breeding See also Flatfish (p. 196-7). Breeds in the spring in relatively shallow water.

Distribution Western Atlantic and Mediterranean.

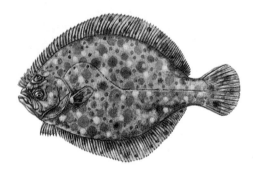

MEGRIM   *Lepidorhombus whiffiagonis*

This small, left-handed flatfish is found in North European waters but rarely in the North Sea, which appears too shallow for the species' lifestyle. The Megrim is quite an important commercial species.

Appearance Length 61 cm; weight 2 kg. Slender body narrows towards the large head with sizable jaws and eyes. If held up to the light, a Megrim's body is almost transparent. Scales are rough to the touch and easily detached.

Feeding Small demersal fishes and crustaceans

Breeding See also Flatfish (p. 196-7). Spawns April–May in deep water. Little study undertaken on development.

Distribution North Atlantic off Ireland and up to Iceland.

SCALDFISH

Arnoglossus laterna

The Scaldfish lives in deep water over sandy ground.

Appearance Length 20 cm; weight 400 g. Light brown body, shaped like that of the Sole (p. 211), with small mouth and large scales set into skin that is easily torn off (as if rinsed away) – hence the fish's common name. This can be seen when a catch is emptied from the trawl – the fish appear naked! Lateral line is curved over the pectoral fins.

Feeding Small fish and invertebrates.

Breeding See also Flatfish (p. 196-7). Spawns in late-spring out in the Atlantic and late summer in the southern North Sea.

Distribution From the Bay of Biscay, north to Norway.

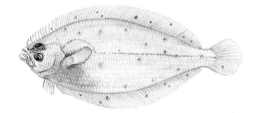

TOPKNOT

Zeugopterus punctatus

Like the Scaldfish (p. 201), this is another small, left-handed flatfish with very spiny scales. It can be found in fairly shallow water over the rough seabed.

Appearance Length 25 cm. Almost round in shape, appearing to be totally surrounded by fins, broken only by the large head and mouth. Scales are thorny and not easily removed. Dark brown in colour, with numerous darker blotches.

Feeding Small fish fry and crustaceans.

Breeding See also Flatfish (p. 196-7). Little is known except that Topknot appears to spawn in shallow, rock-strewn areas with kelp beds.

Distribution From the Cherbourg peninsula up to Norway.

HALIBUT   *Hippoglossus hippoglossus*

The largest-growing of the 'right-handed' flatfish, this powerful, smooth-scaled swimmer is found in deep water and is almost arctic in distribution. It inhabits deep water over rocky seabeds and is much sought after by commercial longliners trying to satisfy the demand of European fish markets.

Appearance Length 245 cm; weight can exceed 250 kg. Dark, greenish-bronze, often with lighter areas. Body long and thick with a wide, strong tail ideal for swimming in tide rips and other areas of strong current.

Feeding
Predates
voraciously on Cod,
Coalfish and other
prime species.

Breeding See also
Flatfish (p. 196-7). Breeds in
winter in deep water, producing millions
of eggs that hatch in two weeks.

Distribution Off the north-western coasts of Norway, Scotland and Ireland.

GREENLAND HALIBUT
Reinhardtius hippoglossoides

Related to the Halibut (see p. 203), the Greenland Halibut is an arctic fish, favouring colder waters than its larger-growing cousin. Both Halibut species frequent deep water which cannot be successfully trawled. These fish are caught by longlining, practised in depths of 500–1,000 m by arctic fleets from many European nations.

Appearance A smaller species than the Halibut: length 100 cm, weight 50 kg at most. Underside has brown coloration. Less symmetrical fin arrangement than the Halibut and an almost straight lateral line.

Feeding Preys on small fish, prawns and demersal invertebrates.

Breeding See also Flatfish (p. 196-7). Spawns in late spring and early summer.

Distribution From arctic waters to northern Scotland and offshore islands.

DAB

Limanda limanda

The Dab is a widely distributed north European flatfish, particularly found in shallow areas with a sandy seabed.

Appearance
Length 25 cm; weight 800 g. Slim, right-handed flatfish with hard scales, especially noticeable when the fish is rubbed by hand from tail to head. Colour variable but a mid-brown predominates, occasionally with lighter blotches. Lateral line is pronounced and curves sharply over the pectoral fin. No nodules on the body, unlike the Plaice and Flounder (see pp. 207–8). Thorn at the beginning of the anal fin.

Feeding Feeds on a wide variety of creatures, including crustaceans, molluscs and small fish.

Breeding See also Flatfish (p. 197–8). Breeds over a protracted period, February–June.

Distribution From the Bay of Biscay to Norway, as well as around Iceland.

LONG ROUGH DAB
Hippoglossoides platessoides

Unrelated to the Dab (see p. 205), this fish grows larger and favours deeper water. It is not a noted food species as the flesh is flaccid and considered lacking in quality.

Appearance Length up to 30 cm. Grey-brown body with a large mouth and no tubercles. Scales are large and rough (hence its common name). Lateral line almost straight; dorsal fin begins above the eyes.

Feeding Crustaceans, molluscs and worms.

Breeding See also Flatfish (p. 196-7). Spawns from April–June.

Distribution Present throughout the temperate and arctic waters of the North Atlantic, particularly from the British Isles across to Iceland.

PLAICE *Pleuronectes platessa*

The Plaice is among the most prized of fish both to the sea anger and commercial trawlerman. It lives in sea areas of soft or sandy ground with a wide range of depth: 10–100 m.

Appearance Length 100 cm; weight 3.5 kg. Wider in the body than the Dab (see p. 205); spattering of orange spots over body and fins. Smooth small scales cover the body which has a ridge of bony nodules on the head, behind the eyes. Lateral line is nearly straight, with only a slight curve over the pectorals. Body is less slimy to the touch than the Flounder (see p.208), which it resembles superficially.

Feeding Feeds on worms, small crustaceans and molluscs, preferring those species with opening shells; mussels are especially popular.

Breeding See also Flatfish (p. 196-7). Plaice breed late winter through to late spring. There is said to evidence of hybridisation between Plaice, Dabs and Flounders.

Distribution From the western Mediterranean up to Norway, Iceland and into the Baltic.

FLOUNDER   *Platichthys flesus*

This is one flatfish that is tolerant of brackish water, such as estuaries and shallow saltwater lagoons that have a freshwater inflow. It is often found far up into the Bream zone of lowland rivers. The cold weather of winter drives them downriver, out to the deeper, warmer sea. Although the Flounder is a right-handed fish, over a quarter of a commercial catch may contain left-handed specimens and many may exhibit colour deviations.

Appearance Length 50 cm; weight 2 kg. Series of bony nodules along the lateral line, beginning behind the gill case. More slightly spiny nodules follow the base line of both dorsal and anal fins. Possible pale orange spots on the body.

Feeding Nocturnal feeder found on mussel and cockle beds. Diet includes worms, larvae, crustaceans and molluscs.

Breeding See also Flatfish (p. 196-7). Breeds March–April in saltwater around 30 m deep.

Distribution Throughout N Atlantic, into arctic waters and down into the Mediterranean and the Black Sea.

LEMON SOLE *Microstomus kitt*

An oval-shaped species of northern waters, it lives over rocky ground in deep water, 25–100 m deep. This is an important commercial fish in Britain and on the Continent. However, Lemon Sole is a name given to a wide range of flatfish by the fish marketing industry, inviting confusion.

Appearance Length 45 cm; weight 500 g. Rich brown colouring is marked with greenish-yellow marbling; body is slimy and the head and mouth noticeably small.

Feeding Invertebrates, especially polychaete worms, and some crustaceans and molluscs.

Breeding See also Flatfish (p. 196-7). Breeds April–July.

Distribution Found from French coast to arctic waters.

WITCH   *Glyptocephalus cynoglossus*

The Witch is an elongated, deep-water flatfish.

Appearance Length 60 cm; weight 500 g. Body is a dull brown-grey with rough scales on the coloured side and a distinct anal thorn. 'Blind' side is a smoky-white hue. Small mouth and a straight lateral line.

Feeding Worms, crustaceans and molluscs.

Breeding See also Flatfish (p.196-7). Breeds in deep, cold water.

Distribution Widespread across the North Atlantic Ocean and arctic waters.

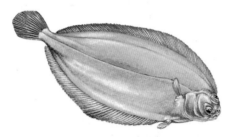

SOLE

Solea solea

This much sought-after species is sometimes called Dover Sole to identify it from the Sand or French Sole *Pegusa lascaris*.

Appearance Length 70 cm; weight 2 kg. Distinctive, elongate body with a blunt, rounded head. Brown in colour with a number of dark blotches in rows on the body and a black spot at the tip of the pectoral fin. Dorsal fin starts in front of the eyes. Two nasal openings on the fish's 'blind' side.

Feeding Nocturnal feeder on small worms, crustaceans and shellfish.

Breeding See also Flatfish (p. 196-7). Spawns in April–June, over sandbanks and even into estuarine water.

Distribution Found around the British Isles, European coast and into the Mediterranean.

SOLENETTE
Buglossidium luteum

This tiny flatfish is similar in appearance and distribution to the Sole (see p. 211).

Appearance Length rarely exceeds 12 cm. Easily recognised by the black rays, distributed evenly through both anal and dorsal fins.

Feeding Small invertebrates and molluscs.

Breeding See also Flatfish (p. 196-7). Spawns offshore; unlike the Sole, it is not found breeding in shallow or estuarine waters.

ANGLERFISH *Lophius piscatorius*

This deep-water species is unmistakable in shape and appearance – it seems to be all head!

Appearance
Length 200 cm;
weight 42 kg.
Body is flattened,
bulbous at the head,
tapering quickly behind the paddle-
like pectoral fins. Dorsal finning is in
four separate divisions: two long, isolated spines in front of the eyes; a single stiff spine; three spines united by a leathery membrane; and a rayed fin before the tail. Outline is broken up by fringing; fleshy protuberances around the mouth and body help to camouflage the fish as it lies buried in a muddy seabed, waiting to pounce on its prey. Mouth is huge, furnished with two rows of sharp, hinged, curved teeth.

Feeding Various other fish, including small members of the cod family, flatfish and sometimes small dogfish.

Breeding March–July, in deep, offshore waters.

Distribution Widespread in north European and Mediterranean waters.

MONKFISH   *Squatina squatina*

An ugly fish of temperate seas, this species appears to be half shark and half skate. It is found in shallow sandy areas, disappearing in winter to warmer, offshore habitats.

Appearance

Length 250 cm; weight 30 kg. Flattened, gristly body, huge paired fins, two dorsal fins, equal in size, and a powerful tail. Grey-brown in colour, there can be spots or streaks of darker hue. Mouth is positioned at the extreme edge of the head, unlike the shark's, to which it is related.

Feeding

Crabs, shellfish and minor demersal fish.

Breeding

Ovoviviparous. Females, depending on size, may contain up to 12 embryos which are said to emerge in the middle of summer.

Distribution

France, north to Denmark and around the British Isles.

GLOSSARY

adipose fin a fleshy appendage without rays found, for instance, on members of the salmon family

alevin a newly spawned salmon or trout

anadromous migrating from the sea into freshwater

barbule fleshy filament growing from the mouth of a fish

ctenoid describing hard scales with a raised point on the rear edge

cusp pointed part of a tooth

cycloid describing scales with a smooth rear edge

demersal living close to the seabed

dorsal upper side of body

dorsal fin fin along the back

elver young eel

fry young fish

gill arch skeletal support for the gills

gill case flap of skin protecting the gills

gill-rakers horny filaments fringing the inner edges of the gill arches

keels typically on mackerel and other members of the tunny family, small finlets dorsally and ventrally placed on the hard ridges running either side of the fish from the base of the tail to the centre of the body

kelt salmon after spawning and before returning to sea

kype hook on the lower jaw of breeding male salmon and trout

larvae newly hatched young fish retaining the yolksac

littoral relating to the shore of the sea or lake

milt semen of a male fish

nictitating membrane membrane that can be drawn across the eye in cartilaginous fish

ocellus/-i a circular patch surrounded by dark spots

ovipositor tube in the female fish through which eggs are deposited within the oviduct, without any placental connection

ovoviviparous producing young that develop from the egg,

parr young salmon or trout between the stages of fry and smolt

pelage colouring of a fish at certain times, for example during breeding

pelagic occurring in the upper layers of the sea

pharyngeal teeth teeth found at the entrance to the throat

redd a hollow made by the female salmon or trout for spawning in

scute protective bony plate

smolt young salmon or trout after the parr stage

snout front of head between eye and upper jaw

swim bladder organ in a fish used to maintain buoyancy

thorn short, thick spine with a hook-shaped curve, very like that found on a rosebush

tubercle small protuberance

vent anus, serving for both excretion and reproduction

viviparous having a primitive placenta joining the eggs to the uterine wall

wings enlarged pectoral fins of skates and rays

INDEX OF ENGLISH NAMES

INDEX OF SCIENTIFIC NAMES